Living with Jezebel

*An In-Depth Look at the Queen of Narcissism, Her
Tactics, and Three Generations of Destruction*

Miko Marsh

Feel free to follow online for updates or other topics at http://www.mikomoments.com or on youtube at Miko Moments channel.

Edited by Cynthia Tucker.

Cover designed by DesignbyBetty89 on Fiverr.

Scriptures quoted are from the Holy Bible King James Version.

Disclaimer: This information should not be substituted for licensed medical, psychological, or spiritual guidance. Please seek the assistance of medical expertise or counseling services if you feel the need to further discuss your personal situation with a certified professional. Any advice you take from this book you agree to do at your own risk without fault or blame to the publisher or author.

Table of Contents

Introduction: Jezebel = Narcissist

"Jezebel!"

If you've ever heard a woman called this, she was likely thought to be a whore. "Slut" is a more familiar but less powerful word used almost in jest nowadays. Whore is the Biblical term and still carries a punch. Every now and then, the name refers to someone who is mean or has some other unfavorable characteristic.

"Narcissist."

If you've heard this term, especially recently, some politicians or overly self-absorbed people may come to mind. This word is used often to describe people who think they're greater than they are. "Egotistical" is a milder word often used to describe someone who is stuck on himself. Usually, we associate it with people who are obsessed with their physical appearance.

Would you be surprised to find out that narcissist is the secular word for Jezebel or a person with a Jezebel spirit? It took me a while to connect the two. I knew the story of Narcissus and the account of Jezebel, but having a sterile and almost primary understanding of how narcissism is defined, I didn't connect the dots for a long time, which is why I didn't think much of it even when I saw strong traits in people. Although my degree is in psychology, we spent very little time discussing narcissism. Basically, I walked away with the idea that narcissists overexaggerate things and believe themselves to be much bigger than they are – much like a fun house mirror. They are extremely self-absorbed, and they long to have others agree with them on how important they are.

I wish we'd had more detailed information about it.

The problem was that, although it had a clinical name and was one of the personality disorders we learned, I was under the impression that it was mild. I thought delusions of grandeur were just confined to their thoughts and dismissed by people who would hear the narcissist speak. It came across as easy to detect and almost benign. We were more worried about the "aggressive" disorders or the ones that made it almost impossible for people to function normally in society. When I worked with individuals with behavioral challenges, narcissism was never a concern. I might work with someone suffering from schizophrenia, oppositional defiant disorder, or bipolar disorder, but I was never concerned that someone might "think too highly of himself." In fact, we were trying to rebuild self-confidence and self-esteem. It was a welcome relief to see people toot their own horns after completing a hard school assignment or after scoring a point. I never had any reason to suspect that narcissistic behavior would be anything more than mildly annoying.

If I had known then what I know now, my whole life might have been changed.

We have a lot of information and stories coming forward now about what narcissism is. We also have people that are teaching on the evil spirit of Jezebel and how it looks in our lives today. What I haven't seen yet is someone explaining the details of Jezebel's life and how her actions compare to the narcissists we often encounter. I will attempt to walk through the account to show what behaviors we can expect from narcissists, examples of tactics they might use, the impact they can have on others, damage done to generations, and what the Bible says we should do regarding them. To reduce confusion on what level of narcissism I mean, I will discuss them as if they are full-blown, 24 hours a day, 7 days a week, cancerous to the core, "malignant narcissists."

Let's first review the account of Narcissus

Depending on which account you take, Narcissus was the extraordinarily beautiful child of a god and a nymph. As a young man, he broke the heart of someone who fell in love with him and was punished by the gods. He looked upon his reflection in the water and fell so in love with himself he eventually died of a broken heart for not being able to be with himself. Eventually, he was changed into a beautiful flower or a beautiful flower took his place – the narcissus flower.

As you can see, it's easy to walk away from this myth believing the worst that a narcissist could be is vain (ex. Vanity Smurf). They love only themselves and are practically oblivious to the rest of the world. If only vanity was the only problem.

Now, let's review the Biblical account of Jezebel

We first hear of Jezebel in I Kings 16. She is a Zidonian princess, daughter of King Ethbaal, and is married to King Ahab, ruler of the Northern Kingdom of Israel. Ahab and Jezebel are the most notorious ruling couple of all the kings and queens of Israel – both kingdoms considered (the kingdom split after Solomon's rule ended). Ahab set up high places to worship the idols Jezebel wanted and allowed her pagan priests to serve in those temples. She began killing off the prophets of the Lord in Israel to wipe out worship to the Lord.

Sometime during their reign, the prophet Elijah declares there will be a drought until he gives word again, which would be three and a half years later. When Elijah returns, he challenges Ahab to a standoff of Divine proportions. The nation gathered for a showdown at Mt. Carmel, which resulted in the Lord raining down fire from Heaven and the death of Jezebel's prophets. Jezebel vowed revenge, Elijah went into hiding, and God told Elijah his plan and gave him the names of the men who would carry it out.

Ahab saw a vineyard he desired near his property and tried to buy it from the owner, Naboth. When Naboth refused, Ahab went home and sulked. Jezebel took matters into her own hands, had Naboth and his sons killed, and told Ahab the vineyard was his. Elijah prophesied to Ahab that since he had allowed Jezebel to commit murder to steal, he, his sons, and Jezebel would be killed. Moreover, his lineage would end.

All of this takes place over approximately a 20-year period. Ahab dies from battle wounds and his son reigns in his place. When we last see Jezebel, we see a captain of the Israelite army, Jehu, furiously riding toward her. He kills the son and heads to kill Jezebel. She paints her face and yells out the window to him. He asks those inside with her which of them is on his side, and three eunuchs hurl Jezebel out of the window to her death.

This seems to be a totally different personality from someone who is just fascinated with his own image. In fact, a summary of Jezebel's life makes you wonder why people associate whoring with her. She just seems like a mean opportunist.

The differences between the superficial description of the narcissist and the outline we get from Jezebel's story are vast. It's no wonder we have difficulty seeing they're the same person. As Christians, we are to look at the whole Bible to learn. We can miss important lessons by not doing a character study. Lessons from the account are important, but understanding the motivation, behavior, or heart (where Scripture gives us insight) of the people doing the actions can help us see what is displayed by others or even ourselves. It allows us the opportunity to check our own actions to see what fruit we're producing, also.

Why did I decide to write about this?

I have a few reasons.

I know people who are still being damaged directly and either aren't ready to do something to stop it or don't know how to begin. Once you've been beaten down often enough, you stop fighting and just hope to ride out the attack.

We aren't helping others by not warning them. Light exposes things that occur in the dark. Many Believers don't consider how much terror and trauma Jezebel caused and may only think of her as an old deposed queen. However, Jesus mentioned her name when sending instructions to the churches in Revelation. She had to have done some major damage to be referenced as someone to actively avoid and put out of our churches today.

Although people are now starting to speak about things that have happened to them, a lot is done quietly because the narcissists in their lives are walking criminals. I have yet to hear about a true Jezebel who has not purposely and repeatedly done things worthy of extended jail time or, in some cases, the death penalty. Their characters demand intrusion and violations of other people's basic rights. Due to the calculated abuse, the victims fear leaving and hope it all goes away, or they just try to wait abusers out until they die. That means that more abuse can and will occur as the perpetrators move on to "fresh meat" who are completely unsuspecting that they are inviting walking demons into their lives.

Talking openly and publicly about this is rarely an easy decision for people. Some have a deep-hidden shame and guilt associated with the memories and results of abuse. Most suffer from some form of posttraumatic stress disorder. The primary reason people do not speak is that, like most abusers and criminals, they threaten their victims never to tell what happened. This means recipients of the abuse can't receive proper healing, and the abuser is free to continue to manipulate and traumatize others. While they are sitting back enjoying our silence, our names are being dragged through the mud, our credibility is being destroyed, we're suffering from long-term wounds, and we're suffering from the paralyzing fear of the anticipated backlash from our abusers if we speak the truth. **The longer we sit in silence afraid to vocalize anything, the longer we are trapped in emotional prisons and unable to connect properly with others who truly care about us.** At some point, it becomes mandatory for those who have been affected to speak up and set the record straight and show people the truth about the person who has been lying to them for years. Sometimes, lies are revealed immediately, and for those who suffered as children, they may not discover the truth until 60 years later.

Speaking out allows us to begin healing properly and protect potential victims. Like so many others, I did not want to bring attention to the things I suffered. I thought I was protecting someone from severe penalties and potential heartache by not bringing things to light or causing embarrassment, although no one gave me even half that consideration. I got tired of trying to hint at the problems, being the bearer of bad news, or being accused of slandering people close to other victims. All my cares, concerns, and considerations blew up in my face, as liars always found a way to twist and contort the truth to punish me. Honestly, I've dealt with enough in life to be able to take quite a bit of pressure. However, when I realized how pervasive narcissistic terror is and could see three generations of people affected, including my own children, I decided it was time to stop wishing evil would cease and become more assertive.

I had no intention of writing this book when I began my study. Originally, I was just going to post a few videos, talk about a few issues, and then be done with the subject altogether. As I began studying more in-depth, I could see how sinister these people are. My notes became this book. As I began to hear people's stories, I felt like part of a community where we were all collectively self-healing, but I was also heartbroken at the levels of anguish people had suffered at the hands of narcissistic parents. I figured that since the Bible has answers, I should study what it has to say on narcissism. Lo, and behold, the Bible had the narcissists' actions laid out in front of me the whole time!

So, as my small contribution to the family of survivors and to those who risk falling prey to these scoundrels, I want to help people understand that Jezebel and narcissists are the same, and what they can expect. Obviously, this will be Scripture heavy because I am examining a person in the Bible; however, I have tried to make this as understandable as possible for someone who has never opened one. This portion of history involves a lot of people with the same names, so I have tried to be clear enough so you can understand which person is being examined at the time. For the sake of simplicity, I will refer to the narcissist as "she" because of the Jezebel equivalent, but narcissists can also be men.

Background

I don't want to concentrate too heavily on the background as is it would be easy to veer off into studying various events, people, and even words and their meanings during this period. I have included a cheat sheet to help keep track of who is whom. Feel free to refer to it.

Kingdom Division

Jacob, one of the patriarchs (early fathers) of the Bible and grandson of Abraham, was renamed Israel by God, so Israelites are descendants of Jacob. Jacob/Israel had 12 sons. Each son is the patriarch of a lineage that would be known as his tribe. For instance, the eldest son, Reuben, is the father of the Reubenites. Levites, from the lineage of the third son, Levi, are the lineage of priests, with high priests coming through the lineage of Aaron, the brother of Moses. Judah's lineage was prophesied to be the royal line and would have the Promised Seed, Jesus Christ. From the time of Creation, people have looked for Christ to come. As Bible genealogy records, the line would come through specific people, including Judah's tribe and King David's bloodline. So, major names in the ancestry of Christ include: Abraham – father of the faith, Jacob/Israel – father of the 12 tribes, Judah – father of the fourth tribe that is the line that would contain kings, David – king whom God promised a dynasty and an Heir to be on the throne forever (millennial kingdom to come).

The first three kings ruled over a unified country. Saul of the tribe of Benjamin was the first king but was rejected as king when he showed he'd rather please men than please God. David was of the tribe of Judah. Solomon, the wisest man in the world, was David's son and the third king. After Solomon, the kingdom of Israel would be divided. The Northern Kingdom was made of 10 tribes and was called Israel. The Southern Kingdom was made of two tribes and called Judah. (The tribe, Judah, was the larger of the two tribes.) All of the people were "Israelites" because they were descendants of Jacob/Israel. However, it is important to keep in mind that at "the time of the kings," Israel is the Northern Kingdom and Judah is the Southern Kingdom. This will be especially important when discussing people who live during the lifetime of others with the same name.

A major theme throughout the Bible is the preservation of the Promised Seed, and the Lord talks about His promise to David that David's heir would inherit the throne. The Kingdom of Judah had this bloodline. The Kingdom of Israel had people who took the opportunity to rule, so family dynasties changed in the Northern Kingdom.

Some of this may seem unnecessary right now, but the background should help with understanding the events, why they are significant, and the response of the Jezebel. If you simply try to read the passages with Jezebel in them quickly, you will miss many of the character traits of a narcissist. I know I did. There actually aren't that many passages written about her. However, she was queen or queen mother for decades. Her influence permitted by Ahab compounded his sins and the sins of the land to the point the Lord destroyed their dynasty and allowed invaders to make war with them. The New Testament names Jezebel as the woman leading people to their deaths and destruction. This is not all-inclusive, but I will talk about some points that stand out to me.

Jezebel's Family Tree

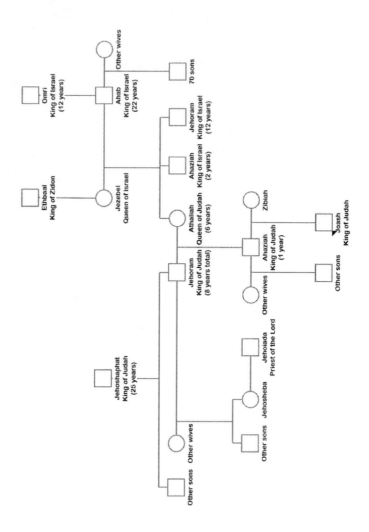

Note: I only added daughters who were named and integral to this study. It is possible that Ahab and Jezebel had more than three children. It is also possible that Ahaziah of Judah had one wife. I had them drawn this way to keep lineages clear.

Names, Meanings, Kings, & Kingdoms

We will cover these as they come up. This is here at the beginning for quick reference to help keep names straight as we go through the life of Jezebel. It's kind of like when we were given a list of vocabulary words we could reference as we were introduced to new literature. If you can keep names and titles straight easily, you won't need to come back to this section.

Elijah – "My God is Yahweh." Elijah is known as one of the major prophets and gave the Word of the Lord to kings in both kingdoms; however, he spent most of his time in the north. Elijah is dedicated to the Lord, and his very name is a continual reminder to the people of Israel and to the king and queen that Elijah was a servant of the One True God. In the NT, John the Baptist is known as the Elijah of the time, preparing people for the coming of Jesus Christ and calling them to repentance. In times future, Elijah will be one of the two witnesses during the tribulation who will testify of the Lord. He is known as the "prophet of fire" due to his answered prayer for the Lord to rain down fire and being taken to Heaven in a whirlwind of fire without having died. Additionally, in the future, he will be able to breathe fire against any who would try to kill him before it is time to be killed.

Asherah – **groves** – Canaanite images of Astarte, Baal's consort. Associated with nature worship, groves were often living trees or tree-like poles meant to be worshiped and/or symbolize female reproduction. She is often seen as the goddess of fertility and earth (nature).

Baal – Has the meanings "lord," "master," "husband," and "giver of life." He was believed to be the god of land and people. He was thought to be the god of agriculture and rain. In many areas, he was considered the sun god. Religious prostitution, sex worship, and human (often child) sacrifice were an integral part of this worship.

Naboth – "fruits" – Murdered so that Ahab could have his vineyard.

Jezebel – Believed to mean "exalted to/for Baal" and "married to Baal." Although she was never officially seen as a ruler, her influence is seen as a reign of turmoil. Her influence includes idolatry, whoredoms, and murder. Her evil influence is strong enough to be mentioned by Christ in Revelation.

Ethbaal – "Toward the idol" or "with Baal." King of the Zidonians and father of Jezebel.

Israel – The Northern Kingdom comprised of 10 tribes of the people Israel; none of these kings followed the lineage of David and are not in the ancestry of Christ.

Judah – The Southern Kingdom comprised of 2 tribes of the people of Israel, with the tribe of Judah numbering most of the land; the lineage of Christ would be preserved through this line.

Jehu – "Jehovah is He."

1. Prophet – The first Jehu we see is in 1 Kings 16; he prophesied the death of King Baasha of Israel and the end of his lineage.

2. Army Captain – the Second Jehu we meet in Israel; he was anointed to destroy Ahab's lineage and destroy Jezebel, and become king of Israel.

Zimri – Reigned as king for seven days before his death; captain in the army of King Elah (son of Baasha) in Israel. Although the prophet Jehu's proclamation would be fulfilled through the destruction of the remainder of Baasha's family through Zimri, there is no record of God instructing Zimri to do so.

Athaliah – "Whom God afflicts." Afflict means greatly troubled or overthrown. She was the daughter of King Ahab and Queen Jezebel of the Kingdom of Israel. She married Jehoram, king of Judah. She is the only woman to ever sit on the throne of Judah as ruler. She usurped the throne after the death of her son, Ahaziah, after killing off all but one person who could lay claim to the throne. She reigned for six years and was killed when the true heir to the throne was revealed to be under protection.

Joash/Jehoash – "Given by the Lord." He was the youngest king of Judah (age 7). He was hidden and kept safe by the priest Jehoiada and his wife, Jehosheba – sister of King Ahaziah & daughter of King Jehoram/Joram. He was given the rightful crown once his grandmother, Athaliah, was killed.

Ahab – "father's brother." He was a king of Israel who reigned for twenty-two years. He married Jezebel, built temples for Baal & Asherah groves, and allowed Jezebel's influence to take over the kingdom. Ahab is known as one of the worst kings in all of Israel's history.

Ahaziah – "Jehovah holds/possesses"

1. In Israel – He was the son of King Ahab and ruled for two years after Ahab was killed in battle – 1 Kings 22:40, 51. He also followed Baal and led Israel into idolatry. He was injured due to a fall, inquired after other gods, and received a proclamation from the Lord through Elijah that he would not recover since he chose to seek the help of another god.

2. In Judah – He was the son of King Jehoram of the Southern Kingdom. He ruled for one year. He was killed during a visit to see King Jehoram in the Northern Kingdom. Jehu was on his way to slay Jehoram according to the Word of the Lord. Jehu shot Jehoram with an arrow, and he was placed in Naboth's field to die. Ahaziah witnessed the death, attempted to flee, and was killed also.

Jehoram – "Jehovah is exalted."

1. In Israel – He was the second son of King Ahab to rule, also called Joram. He became king upon the death of his brother, Ahaziah, because Ahaziah had no sons to succeed him. He ruled for twelve years as king and was killed by Jehu, his army captain, when the Lord sent word to exact divine judgment on Ahab's lineage as prophesied by Elijah about seventeen years earlier.

2. In Judah – He was the son of King Jehoshaphat. Jehoshaphat was not dead when Jehoram became king (2 Kings 8:16). He ruled for eight years and as a contemporary/at the same time as Jehoram in the Northern Kingdom. He married Athaliah, daughter of Ahab and Jezebel of the Northern Kingdom (2 Kings 8:18), possibly as a way

to unite the kingdoms again. Upon his death, his son, Ahaziah, became king.

Israel (Northern Kingdom)	Judah (Southern Kingdom)
Zimri (kills Elah) ruled 7 days – new line	Jehoshaphat (25 years) – allowed son to co-reign with him
Omri (12 years) – new line	
Ahab, son of Omri (22 years) & Jezebel	
Ahaziah, son of Ahab (2 years)	
Jehoram/Joram, son of Ahab (12 years)	Jehoram, son of Jehoshaphat (8 years total)
Jehu – new line	Ahaziah, son of Jehoram (1 year)
	Athaliah, wife of Jehoram/grandmother of Joash/daughter of Jezebel (6 years)
	Joash/Jehoash, son and rightful heir of Ahaziah

Jezebel Enters Israel

1 Kings 16:28-34

"[31]And it came to pass, as if it had been a light thing for him to walk in the sins of Jeroboam the son of Nebat, that he took to wife Jezebel the daughter of Ethbaal king of the Zidonians, and went and served Baal, and worshipped him. [32]And he reared up an altar for Baal in the house of Baal, which he had built in Samaria. [33]And Ahab made a grove; and Ahab did more to provoke the Lord God of Israel to anger than all the kings of Israel that were before him. [34]In his days did Hiel the Bethelite build Jericho: he laid the foundation thereof in Abiram his firstborn, and set up the gates thereof in his youngest son Segub, according to the word of the Lord, which he spake by Joshua the son of Nun." – 1 Kings 16:31-34

What we see here:

King Ahab (enabler) overview
Who is Jezebel?
Baal worship and groves/Ashtoreth (goddess of Zidonians – 1 Kings 11:5)
Wickedness increased in the land
Jezebel is religious

Ahab was already doing wickedness in the sight of the Lord. To follow in the ways of Jeroboam is a reference to him bringing and allowing idols/false god worship in the kingdom. Israel was meant to be a theocracy in which God was the ruler. They already had a code of laws known as the Law of Moses that had been presented to them hundreds of years before. The people demanded a king to be like other nations during the time of the judges. Samuel warned them of the problems that would come with a king other than God, but the people rejected God as their King. Once Israel had a king in place, the king had certain obligations to follow since the people tend to follow the direction of its leadership. These rules included not marrying foreign women, as they were outside the covenant and would turn the kings' hearts away from the Lord. Another was not to

19

engage in idolatry or permit it, as turning from the Lord would bring the curses mentioned in the Law that all Israelites were to follow. The Israelite Kingdom was divided due to Solomon's disobedience (1 Kings 11), which is how the Northern Kingdom of Israel came into being. Ahab is only six kings past Jeroboam (the first king of Israel, the Northern Kingdom) and barely seventy years into the kingdom division. Therefore, there still could have been people alive who lived during the United Kingdom. Basically, not enough time had passed that the nation couldn't remember the laws or see the problems that arose from disobedience.

Ahab, the Enabler:

This lets us see that for all of Jezebel's compounded sins, Ahab was a willing participant. **He is the enabler**. The scripture says Ahab behaved "as if it were a light thing…" This marriage was a major move gone wrong, as Jezebel begins to change things from the beginning. Marrying Jezebel, erecting idols for her to lead the nation into false god worship, and permitting and/or enforcing all the evil Jezebel brought has earned him the title of "worst king in all of Israelite kingdom history," because he kindled the Lord's anger through these actions.

Enablers will do the narcissist's bidding. They are not forced into their agreements. Although the narcissist gets the most enjoyment or benefit from the enabler's compliance, the enabler will go along because there is some reward in it for themselves even if it is small. In everyday life, this is the person who continues to allow the narcissist to do what shouldn't be done. They know the action is wrong, but they either don't try to stop it or they are active participants. They are "guilty by association."

Sometimes, the enabler is quiet and pretends he doesn't see what is happening, such as when a mother-in-law takes it upon herself to make repeated jabs/insults to the daughter-in-law. Instead of standing up for the wife, the husband ignores the words, laughs with his mother, or tells his wife that she's too sensitive. Other times, the enabler can act as the henchman. The narcissist may complain about what someone else is doing or saying (it usually isn't true or is greatly exaggerated), and the henchman threatens the perceived offender or carries out punishments the narcissist feels are appropriate. These could include calling someone to tell her what she should do for the narcissist or a parent returning from a long business trip and informed he needs to spank his child months after the "disobedience" took place, which causes the child to be punished twice for a one-time act.

Jezebel, the Narcissist:

Jezebel is a Zidonian princess and the daughter of Ethbaal. This was a marriage of politics and power – not of love. The name Ethbaal means "with Baal." Her father would have taught her the ways of their people, including their worship. Names often have strong meaning to people, and there is no exception here. While there is some disagreement about the exact meaning of her name, many believe the syllables of her name mean "exalted to/for Baal." Some see a negative in her name in front of a marriage to Baal to be interpreted as "unmarriable" and reserved for Baal. I think the consensus is that her name shows that she is "married to Baal." By her being married to her god, she is actually unavailable to her husband because her first devotion is to her god. She is trained in the ways of worship and ritualistic practices before she steps one foot on Israelite soil. There is no indication that she has any love for Ahab.

Narcissists do not love people. They participate in relationships as a way to gain control. Power is motivation, and they go in already dedicated to something or someone (themselves) else. This is easy to see when you pour your heart out, and the narcissist says, "mm hmm" all through your conversation or is unable to sympathize with you and moves on to a topic about themselves after blowing off your concerns and pains. There is no human or emotional connection.

The narcissist is virtually "unmarriable" also. She may get married, but she never attaches to anyone. She is totally sold out to do evil and is always thinking of ways to get what she wants.

Baal Worship

The history of Baal worship is the belief that the actions of the gods dictated what would happen on earth. Since Baal is thought to be the god of rain, when there was a dry or winter season, he was under the earth or temporarily sleeping or defeated. When lesser gods would help resuscitate him, he would return to bring rain to the land. Actions of people would help to give him strength and encourage him to have sex with Ashtoreth to bring forth crops and abundant harvest. These sexual, magic rituals usually occurred in what the Bible refers to as high places, or in temples that housed priests and/or temple prostitutes. Child sacrifice was sometimes practiced.

Baal and Asherah worship was big in foreign lands. Asherah were groves and considered the female goddess and counterpart to Baal. When the gods had sex, good things happened for the land, as it would bring conditions ripe for seeding and harvest. These were strictly forbidden, yet Ahab began to serve Baal and had temples and groves built for Jezebel. Their practices were continual, and the participants were continually doing whatever tasks they believed would satiate the appetite of their god.

Jezebel is highly religious:

Don't confuse being "religious" with being "saved." People will do all sorts of things in the name of their religion. Jezebel was a die-hard religious fanatic. She was completely sold out to her god and made sure she did not forsake her beliefs when she entered this arranged marriage. In fact, she wanted everyone else to convert to her religion. From this passage, we can see that she would not leave her ways behind her even though she knew she was marrying into what was supposed to be a theocracy. Instead of one person converting to the land, she brought her beliefs in and would eventually expect the land to convert for her.

Narcissists tend to be very religious and love religious activity because it makes them appear "spiritual" and benevolent, and it is a good place to become a leader while twisting the teachings of the religion. However, a tree is known by its fruit. If that person does not live what they teach on a consistent basis and is going out of her way to change meanings, then you can tell the person is only using the religion as a cover.

Wickedness compounded:

As influence began to trickle down to the people, the wickedness of the land increased. A man named Hiel decided to reconstruct Jericho, which had been laid waste since the march around the city in the book of Joshua. There was a curse prophesied that the man who chose to rebuild the city would lose his sons in the construction. Until the point Jezebel was in the area, all had heeded the warning from God to leave the city in ruins for a permanent remembrance of the miraculous conquest of Jericho. Hiel's sons died in the construction project.

Narcissists tend to have an evil energy around themselves. I call it a "cloud of gloom" looming over them. It's a heaviness that is so thick it has a presence. You can feel your spirit getting weighed down, and you long for the narcissist to be positive or just go away. You notice people around her are doing questionable activities. The influence will likely cause you to behave in ways you wouldn't normally also. For instance, you may curse or threaten people more, or you may increase how often you gossip about people.

Enter Elijah, the Lord's Prophet to the King

1 Kings 17

Elijah, the proclamation, and the significance

"[1]And Elijah the Tishbite, who was of the inhabitants of Gilead, said unto Ahab, As the Lord God of Israel liveth, before whom I stand, there shall not be dew nor rain these years, but according to my word." – 1 Kings 17:1

Elijah – means "my God is Yahweh." Elijah is known as one of the major prophets and gave the Word of the Lord to kings in both kingdoms. Not much is known of his background, and he bursts onto the scene with a proclamation of impending drought. Elijah is dedicated to the Lord, and his very name is a continual reminder to the people of Israel and to the king and queen that Elijah was a servant of the One True God. In the New Testament, John the Baptist is known as the Elijah of the time, preparing people for the coming of Jesus Christ and calling people to repentance. In times future, Elijah will be one of the two witnesses during the tribulation who will testify of the Lord. He is known as the "prophet of fire" due to his answered prayer for the Lord to rain down fire and being taken to Heaven in a whirlwind of fire without having died. Additionally, in the future, he will be able to breathe fire against any who try to kill him before it is time to be killed.

The reason Elijah prayed for no rain was not simply because of Baal. After the Israelites chose to enter into covenant with the Lord to be His people, they were given a Law that included blessings for obedience and curses for disobedience, much the same way a parent would give privileges to a child for doing as he should and punishments for breaking the rules. The Lord usually waited a long period of time before sending curses, giving people time to repent. He would send prophets and Godly leaders to the people to remind them of their covenant, to remind them of Who God is and what He did, and to warn people to turn from their ways.

"¹³And it shall come to pass, if ye shall hearken diligently unto my commandments which I command you this day, to love the Lord your God, and to serve him with all your heart and with all your soul, ¹⁴That I will give you the rain of your land in his due season, the first rain and the latter rain, that thou mayest gather in thy corn, and thy wine, and thine oil. ¹⁵And I will send grass in thy fields for thy cattle, that thou mayest eat and be full. ¹⁶*Take heed to yourselves, that your heart be not deceived, and ye turn aside, and serve other gods, and worship them*; ¹⁷And then the Lord's wrath be kindled against you, and *he shut up the heaven, that there be no rain*, and that the land yield not her fruit; and lest ye perish quickly from off the good land which the Lord giveth you." – Deuteronomy 11:13-17

The Lord warned that if they turned from Him to worship other gods, He would withhold rain. A drought that lasted for a long time would eventually lead to starvation. Israelites weren't always perfect in obedience, but a strong word or admonition from the Lord generally helped people's hearts return to Him. When Jezebel brought her prophets and gods and had temples built to encourage people to bow to these idols, the land became a cesspool for Baal worship. Therefore, Elijah prayed that God fulfill His warning as divine discipline to the people of Israel to convict them of their sins to bring them back to the Lord as well as an open display of power against the idol, Baal.

Life on the run:

The proclamation was issued in 1 Kings 17:1. Immediately in the next verse, we see that God told Elijah to hide himself and tells him to live by a brook. There ravens bring him food, and he drinks from the brook until it dries up. He is then instructed to go to Zidon, Jezebel's hometown, where a widow, poorer than dirt poor, would feed and care for him. The widow trusts Elijah's words to the point she shares her last meal. The Lord provides enough meal and oil to prepare their daily sustenance for the remainder of the drought. Sometime during the famine, the widow's son falls sick and dies. Elijah prays, and the boy is brought back to life. The widow comes to full faith in the Lord.

What we see here:

Elijah suffered with the rest of the Israelites during the drought. He experienced severe hunger and thirst for the same three years. He was totally dependent on God to get him through it. Elijah spent much of his time on the run hiding in Jezebel's hometown, which meant that he risked being identified and sent back to Israel or subjected to whatever the Zidonians would have done to him had he been caught. Elijah had not done anything illegal. In fact, he addressed the king and simply said what God instructed him to say, but he was instructed to hide because of the anger that would start from the proclamation and build as people realized it would not rain and affected crops, animals, and people.

In the midst of the famine, God is showing mercy…to His enemies. The widow lived in Zidon, a land plagued with idol worship. She is introduced to a man who tells her about the one true God. She lives a miracle within a miracle by the fact that this same God Who shut up the heavens is providing her daily bread when not too long before, she was preparing to serve the last meal so she and her son could eat and then starve to death. God sent the prophet into a land that hates the Lord to introduce Him to this widow. When her son dies, God shows mercy again by bringing him back to life. The widow willingly chooses to believe in the Lord, which shows us that the Lord gives all people opportunity to believe and turn to Him.

The widow's response will be important to remember.

Jezebel Is a Murderer at Heart

1 Kings 18:1-16

1 Kings 18 is a fairly long passage to write here, so if you're unfamiliar and want to read every word. Please do so. In summary (verses 1–16), the Lord told Elijah to appear before Ahab because the Lord was going to bring back the rain. We learn a man named Obadiah ("servant of Jehovah") works in or oversees affairs in Ahab's house and hid one hundred prophets of the Lord in caves when Jezebel issued a demand for their slaughter. The land is experiencing a severe famine since it hadn't rained in three years. Ahab ordered Obadiah to search far and wide to find water and grass to feed the animals.

While out, Obadiah runs into Elijah and is instructed to tell Ahab to meet him. Elijah assures Obadiah that he will not disappear. We learn there has been an international manhunt for Elijah.

While Jezebel is not the subject of this chapter, we see several things that are a result of her actions:

Importance of the enabler
Introduces fear to those living in the household
Hatred for all things righteous and of God
Murderous nature of the narcissist
Stalking persistence

The enabler is key

Jezebel lives in a patriarchal society. Ahab is the final authority before God. Men led the households and determined the direction of the family. Kings led the nation and determined the direction of the nation. Nothing Jezebel wants can be done without the king's permission. She is outside the covenant and refuses to submit to the Law of God. Everything that she is permitted to do, ultimately, rests on the shoulders of Ahab and is his fault. Even though Jezebel is the reason behind what is going on, she is not the responsible party. Ultimately, God will deal with her for what she does, but she is literally the person pulling the strings behind the curtain. The enabler is the fall guy because he has to say, "yes" or "no" to what happens and must accept the repercussions of his choices. The enabler is not clueless to what is going on. He is very much aware of what is going on, but he generally benefits somehow from her plots. An enabler could be anyone, including a former victim; however, an enabler is usually someone who is in the position to give something of high value to the narcissist – like the ability to support her lifestyle desires.

In today's society, this is very beneficial to the narcissist. It's similar to the person who types up the news report that will be read live over the air. The reporter reads the report that was written by someone else. However, if it's an inflammatory statement, the reporter catches the backlash because he's the one who said it. He had the option to read, not read, or correct it at the time and didn't, but the behind-the-scenes writer is the one who caused the upset.

Your narcissists may insist you put a bill in your name before you deploy so that any payment issues must be delayed because you are in the service. While you're gone, they rack up an enormous amount of debt in your name, which damages your credit but requires you to make payments. Your enabler might allow an abusive girlfriend/boyfriend/relative to physically or sexually injure you by continuing to expose you to that person despite your objection and requests to not go. Sometimes, the enabler gets something out of it like bills paid, but it could be just to get the narcissist to shut up. If the narcissist is focused on you, then the enabler has a moment without being the target.

Normal people are uncomfortable living with them:

Obadiah is governor of the house. He is a devoted servant of the Lord, yet after he does his chores for the household, he has to steal away to protect the lives of those who are actually supposed to be in the land. He has to find a way to get water and bread to one hundred men so they don't die of starvation or are killed due to Jezebel's orders. We can see the great pressure Obadiah feels to do what's right in an openly hostile and oppressive home by the fact that he tells Elijah that if he tells Ahab that he saw the prophet, and the prophet leaves, Obadiah would be killed. Obadiah isn't just thinking of himself but also of the other prophets he's now taken the responsibility of saving.

Narcissists make people hate living with them. While the threat of murder may not hang in the air, narcissists seem to always be after someone. There is no peace in the home, so the resident must always be on guard. The victims often express feeling as if they're walking on eggshells or through a minefield. Many people feel they can't truly be themselves even in homes where the parent is the narcissist. Some part of themselves that they dearly love must be hidden away so the narcissistic parent doesn't kill it – usually a dream, such as a career in a field the parent doesn't want the child to pursue or a talent, such as art. This usually happens after they have witnessed the child's talent. The parent does this when the child enthusiastically presents the idea only to have it shot down, stomped on, and ground to powder.

Jezebels hate anything associated with the Lord:

Jezebel issued an order for the slaughter of the prophets of the Lord – not just prophets (she had prophets also) – prophets of the Lord. It wasn't enough for her to bring in Baal and Asherah worship. She wanted to eliminate anyone who would talk about the Lord and His Word. Prophets of the Old Testament didn't just walk around telling people what the future held. The job of prophets was similar to that of a pastor and evangelist. They reminded people of the commandments of God, exhorted people to repent of their sins to return to God, and confronted people about their sins. Jezebel didn't want prophets of the Lord around because they were a continual reminder that she was doing everything God hated. If prophets were permitted to speak openly, someone might cause her to be removed from her throne, evicted from the land, or even stoned to death for her idolatry. Her idols would be cast down and groves destroyed. Ahab might have a change of heart and try to obey God. Jezebel wanted to cut off the voices for God and silence any others who might consider speaking up. Jezebels do not recognize that they are actually fighting the Lord Himself and not the person living for God. Jesus told Saul/Paul that persecution of Believers is actually persecution of Himself.

This plays out in a variety of ways. A Christian is always seen as an enemy to a narcissist, especially in the church. Most other religions are tolerated, but true Christianity always cuts the heart of a narcissist because we use the objective Word of the Bible as a standard by which everyone, including ourselves, must be judged. The Bible states that we must surrender our will and submit to the One Who made us. We are to be servants, have a humble heart, love others, show compassion, etc. None of these things appeal to the narcissist and are likely to repulse her because Jezebel makes her own gods. She lives to serve self. She doesn't want to submit to anyone and treats everyone as if they owe her.

A narcissist may tell people that someone is "too religious" or that the person is trying to make them all think they're going to hell. She will use the person's faith as a way to turn others against him. "It doesn't take all that to be a Christian." You may be discredited as not knowing anything because you don't have a platform or certain degree or "used to…" do something in the past. She will use whatever tactic available to separate those doing right from herself and those she wishes to control to minimize the chance that they will hear and feel conviction about their sins.

Narcissists do not wish to be exposed for the crimes and evil they commit; therefore, they attempt to silence anyone who can shed light on them.

Narcissists are murderers at heart

Jezebel demanded the deaths of all the Lord's prophets. The likelihood that all of these prophets personally offended Jezebel or went to the palace and told her to repent is about zero. They had specific assignments, and we usually only see one primary prophet given an occasional word for anyone, especially the king. She wanted them dead because she hated them and Who they represented. In the sermon on the mount, Jesus taught us hating people in our hearts makes us murderers at heart even though we haven't committed the physical deed. Jezebel had an active order for murder and had no problem displaying her hatred.

There was no love between Jezebel and Ahab. Their marriage was a business/political deal. Narcissists do not love. They hate. If they believe they can get away with it, they will kill, or rather, put it in someone else's mind to do the killing to avoid have a direct tie to the murder. They might suggest a friend drive a vehicle over someone, find a way to poison the person, or concoct a story to enrage someone enough to attack or kill the "offender." Although the narcissist does hate you enough to want your death, she may settle for putting you away permanently, such as having you sent to jail on trumped-up charges. Your voice is still muffled since people are less likely to listen to you once you've been arrested.

Persistent Stalker/Personal Vendetta:

"[10]As the Lord thy God liveth, there is no nation or kingdom, whither my lord hath not sent to seek thee: and when they said, He is not there; he took an oath of the kingdom and nation, that they found thee not." – 1 Kings 18:10

Obadiah tells Elijah of the great lengths Ahab has gone to find Elijah during the years of the drought – even to the point of making other nations swear they did not know Elijah's location.

If you have personally called the Jezebel on her faults, embarrassed/upstaged her, or are in the position to open the eyes of her enabler and/or victims, she will use any and every effort to destroy you. Jezebel focused on Elijah because Elijah had Ahab's attention, was influential in the land, and was showing her god to be powerless. Everything Jezebel had was at risk of slipping from her clutches. Although none of this would have been an issue if Jezebel had simply let the nation be without deciding the entire nation needed to change to bend to her will, she saw Elijah as a personal threat to her. For that, she wanted Elijah destroyed…as if that would somehow stop God from being God.

With social media, it is easier to follow, monitor, and harass people through cyberstalking. Narcissists love to know what you're doing. They are snoops, super spies, and suspicious. On a lesser scale, they will go through your mail, messages, drawers, send people to "check/report on you," and use any excuse to find out anything they can to use against you later. As in the passage, people were sent into neighboring nations and interrogated about Elijah's whereabouts. They want to know what you're doing, with whom, how, for how long, where, etc. Even if they manage to chase you away, they are still looking to find you and destroy you with a long arm. You might have rumors started about you, calls to your job, family members questioned, harassing phone calls and messages, emails/texts/letters, and so forth. This might not have the immediate desire of killing you or driving you to suicide, but the objective is to cause you continual upset. Some people have experienced "gangstalking," which means having multiple people monitor them.

Many people see this in relationships. For instance, a woman who has married the "son-husband" (the child the narcissistic mother treats as her husband) will be targeted until she is divorced from the man the narcissist raised to support her and take care of her for all of her life.

Battle of the Gods

1 Kings 18:17-46

If you are familiar with this passage, you might want to skip down to the "what we see in this passage" section.

Elijah meets Ahab. He asks Elijah if he's the one causing Israel so much trouble. (Trouble here indicates a problem that is so severe it can only be solved by the death of the troublemaker.) Elijah tells him it is Ahab, his father's house, and they (the household) who are causing the trouble, because they've gone astray from the Lord to worship Baal and have led Israel astray also. He instructs Ahab to gather everyone in the nation to Mt. Carmel and to bring all 450 prophets of Baal and 400 prophets of groves/Asherah that have been dining at Jezebel's table. Ahab obeyed.

Elijah asked the people to decide who to serve as god. He said he was 1 prophet against 450 prophets.

The challenge: two gods, two altars, two bulls for sacrifice, and prophets to represent their gods to pray. The God Who answers by fire is God and would be served. The people accepted the challenge. (Who wouldn't want to worship Someone Who throws fire from the sky?)

Elijah tells the Baal prophets to go first, set up their sacrifice, don't light it, and call upon their god. For hours they called, jumped around, and got on the altar. Elijah began mocking them around noon telling them to scream louder. Maybe their god couldn't hear because he was talking to someone else, using the bathroom, on a long trip, or in a deep sleep. The prophets got louder and began cutting themselves with sharp items until they were covered in blood. The Bible says it "gushed" out of them. They spent from morning until evening trying to get Baal to answer.

Elijah called Israel closer, rebuilt one of the Lord's damaged altars, built a trench around the altar, and doused the sacrifice, altar, and trenches with four barrels of water so that it was soaked and water ran into the sides. Elijah prayed a simple prayer, and the Lord sent fire that burned the sacrifice and wood, and dried up the water in the trench. When the people saw it, they began worshiping the Lord.

The prophets of Baal were rounded up and killed. Elijah told Ahab to go eat and drink and prepare for a big rain. Elijah prayed for rain and sent his servant to tell Ahab to leave in his chariot so that he didn't get caught in the downpour. The Lord then moves Elijah, and he outruns the chariot.

Jezebel is not present, but we can still see her representatives and her influence.

What we see here:

Jezebel's prophets are feasting
Enabler doesn't target you on his own
Bloody scene
Miracles

Jezebel's table:

The entire nation faced a famine that dried up fresh water and was causing the starvation of both animals and people, and Jezebel isn't suffering. She is still providing well for her false prophets. They remain in her company. Remember, the Lord's prophets who yet remain alive are struggling to survive on bread and water being provided to them by Obadiah while her prophets are at the queen's table eating as if they are royalty. This isn't because she necessarily likes them. She's making sure the people who perform rituals for her god and goddess are satisfied. From the jumping around and all-day struggle to get Baal to answer, you could guess she wants them to stay strong for all the rituals they perform.

Although this may not be major to some, narcissists like to have control over the most minute details – including dictating when you can eat and what food you can access. This would be like giving you a couple of hot dogs, telling you not to eat past a certain time while enjoying $100 meals to treat your sister to dinner, and then expecting you to be thankful for crumbs.

The enabler isn't after you:

Ahab had the opportunity to kill Elijah on sight but didn't. Not only did he not attempt to even capture Elijah, he listened and did everything Elijah instructed without so much as an objection or question about why he should comply. This could be because the enabler has a personality that is more of a follower or a "yes man." It's more likely that Ahab knew that killing Elijah was wrong, wouldn't solve his problems, and ultimately would bring problems on himself. Elijah spoke the truth, and Ahab knew it.

Oftentimes the enabler will leave you alone or even be somewhat enjoyable company when it's just you and the enabler talking. You can see him as a real person and get to know more about him. When the narcissist is present, the enabler insults you, mocks you, and may even carry out orders to beat you. The narcissist wants to keep you far away from each other because your truth and ability to show the enabler what's really going on would be the narcissist's undoing. She needs to keep him in her grasp.

Graphic scene of the prophets

The behavior of the prophets shows us a glimpse of their rituals for worship. While Baal worship involves sexual deviance/temple prostitution, which they believed encouraged the gods to have sex, make rain, and give a harvest, it also involves child sacrifice (Jeremiah 19:5). The prophets were willing to do anything they could to get a response from their god – including mutilating themselves. Their worship involves extreme harm to self to help empower or to get an answer from their god, so killing someone else would be easier because it causes no pain to themselves. These activities are forbidden by the Lord. The Bible doesn't specify what happened during the three years, but it makes you wonder to what extent they went trying to get it to rain.

The prophets were not just killed for having a different belief. This was a Divine sentencing. For starters, the Lord's prophets were killed for doing what they were instructed in their own land because Jezebel wanted them dead to make room for her gods. Deuteronomy 13, in the Law of Moses, instructed Israelites to put to death the prophets leading the people to worship another god. These people had witnessed with their own eyes the miracles of the Lord, so it was a huge insult to have them turn around and say something they could make with their hands is their god.

Fire from Heaven:

This is the central focus of this chapter. There is undeniable proof that the Lord is God. Thousands of people witnessed the God challenge.

Rain:

The Lord first sends down fire, which laps up the water on the altar. He then sends a downpour of rain.

"[35]When heaven is shut up, and there is no rain, because they have sinned against thee; if they pray toward this place, and confess thy name, and turn from their sin, when thou afflictest them: [36]Then hear thou in heaven, and forgive the sin of thy servants, and of thy people Israel, that thou teach them the good way wherein they should walk, and give rain upon thy land, which thou hast given to thy people for an inheritance." – 1 Kings 8:35-36, from the prayer of King Solomon at the temple dedication in Jerusalem.

The rain for which Elijah prayed returned after the confession of the people that the Lord is God and after they put down the false prophets of idols. Again, it was not a random miracle that Elijah thought up out of thin air. It was in the Law of Moses as a judgment upon the land for turning to idolatry and an answer to prayer for returning to Him. This would be recorded in the Scriptures for the king to see, especially since the rulers of the Northern Kingdom did not want their inhabitants to go to the Southern Kingdom to worship at the rightful temple.

This showdown would be a devastating blow to Jezebel. Her life and identity were wrapped up in this god, and the Lord had just proved Baal to be impotent and unable to do anything. At least at one unified time, all of the kingdom acknowledged openly that the Lord is God, and she couldn't make people forget it. Not only was it shown that Baal isn't god, her prophets had been wiped out.

All the events here set the stage for chapter 19.

Jezebel Demands Elijah's Death/Elijah's Great Depression

1 Kings 19

Most of this chapter is not Jezebel's conversation or actions but what happened because of one sentence from her. This passage is key. It shows a scene of life with a narcissist, her enabler, and her victim. Every victim of a narcissist understands this passage all too well. This plays out in victims' lives multiple times on many levels. Sometimes, it's so subtle, outsiders look at us as if we're blowing things out of proportion. Sometimes, it's so outrageous, that outsiders will step between the narcissist and the victim in order to protect the victim and bring some sort of justice to the narcissist (ex. have her arrested).

"¹And Ahab told Jezebel all that Elijah had done, and withal how he had slain all the prophets with the sword. ²**Then Jezebel sent a messenger unto Elijah, saying, So let the gods do to me, and more also, if I make not thy life as the life of one of them by to morrow about this time**. ³And when he saw that, he arose, and went for his life, and came to Beersheba, which belongeth to Judah, and left his servant there. ⁴But he himself went a day's journey into the wilderness, and came and sat down under a juniper tree: and he requested for himself that he might die; and said, 'It is enough; now, O Lord, take away my life; for I am not better than my fathers.' ⁵And as he lay and slept under a juniper tree, behold, then an angel touched him, and said unto him, 'Arise and eat.'" – 1 Kings 19:1-5

What we see here:

The report
The enabler gets out of the way to let her fly off the handle
Gaslighting/Facts and proof are ignored
Narcissistic injury
Narcissistic rage (irrational, lashing out, threats, cursing, desires for total annihilation)
PTSD, hopelessness, and depression

37

The report:

Jezebel feels she must know everything that is going on within her reach, especially if it affects her directly. She makes sure there is someone to give her an update. In this case, it is her husband. We see that the report tells of what "Elijah did" and how Elijah killed her prophets. Technically, Elijah was obeying the Lord. Yes, Elijah called the contest, but Ahab let it happen. Ahab probably felt he had the upper hand since the prophet gave him what would seem to be an advantage – a battle in a "high place" and a battle to send down fire, which should be simple for a "sun god." Elijah knew the prayer that Solomon had prayed and had answered that if the Lord had sent a drought, to hear the people when they repented and turned back to Him. The Lord had told him that it was time to send rain, so when the people repented and worshiped Him, God would answer. The display was to solidify in the Israelites' hearts Who He is. The report seems to leave out the miracle and the Lord being God.

When the report gets back, summarized, interpreted, whatever, you're going to be the center of the report. You're also going to be the cause of whatever happened regardless of the reason. What you do could have been just shy of a miracle and got the attention of the whole world. It's a problem because your good attention is seen as bad attention for your narcissist. They never want you to succeed.

The enabler makes sure you're the scapegoat:

The glaringly obvious facts don't seem to matter here. It's not shown as part of the conversation, but it doesn't seem that Ahab bothered to accept an ounce of responsibility for anything. Ahab is king, yet he is "reporting" to Jezebel. Ahab agreed to the showdown at Mt. Carmel. Ahab was ringside to witness the complete and utter failure of Jezebel's prophets to get their god to do a single thing while the Lord flung fire from the sky right in front of him. Ahab witnessed that everything happened just as Elijah said down to the point he had time to eat, drink, and avoid being stranded in a flash flood in the first rain in over three years of drought. Ahab is an Israelite and should know the history of the kings and the Law. Ahab saw the people worship God and should have been right on his face with the rest of the people. Despite everything he saw firsthand, he laid blame at Elijah's feet and allowed Jezebel to lose her mind and go on a rampage. Instead of putting his foot down to tell her it's enough or not to possibly anger the Lord Who had just scorched stone to turn His wrath on them, he chose to fear her wrath more than the Lord he'd just witnessed as the true God.

Enablers will move out of the way to let the narcissist attack you instead of taking ownership for their roles, standing up for you and what's right, or just preventing more problems by not giving her the permission to do any more damage. They will avoid short-term discomfort on the receiving end of Jezebel's anger by throwing you under the bus and walking away to let you catch the heat.

Gaslighting – Facts and proof meaning nothing to Jezebel:

You would think that upon hearing the day's events, Jezebel would take a moment to reflect on the whole picture...maybe even think about the meaning of life. Baal was supposed to control the rain, and the Lord made the rain stop by Elijah's word. They searched high and low for Elijah and couldn't find him until he revealed himself for a battle of the gods. Baal hadn't answered them all these years regardless of the rituals and sacrifices they performed. The Lord proved Himself in front of the people by sending down fire in front of thousands and then made it rain. She could see, hear, smell, touch, and taste the rain and also saw that none of her prophets returned. Jezebel ignores *all* of it to focus on making Elijah the problem. Her position is that Elijah has caused all her problems. The widow in Zidon confessed the Lord is God, yet this Zidonian living in the land that has access to the history of the Lord and witness to miracles still refuses to acknowledge the Lord as God.

As far as Jezebel is concerned, "You didn't see what you clearly just saw." This is a gaslighting. It's also known as "crazy-making." You and the narcissist both know something very specific occurred, and the narcissist will look you dead in the eyes and tell you that it didn't happen. For example, it can be as simple as the narcissist moving an item and lying about it when you can't find it. There are usually numerous small things done at different times to make the person question what they know and begin to doubt themselves, which tends to lead to dependence on the narcissist. It can even lead to loss of self-worth and a feeling of inadequacy.

If witnessing first-hand miracles didn't impact Jezebel enough to even acknowledge the truth of what happened, your proof has far less meaning to your Jezebel. The narcissist makes all accounts about herself, through her eyes, and tells her narrative as if she's in a parallel universe. Nothing you say or do is going to change her mind. It will only make her hate you more for making her look incompetent. Facts are irrelevant to the narcissist if she can't benefit from them.

Narcissistic Injury:

Jezebel is irrational in her logic. She is cunning, but she doesn't seem to piece things together properly. Even though Elijah never said a word to her, sent a message to her, called for her, or even mentioned her name, Jezebel took everything personally. If you remember, in chapter 17, Elijah appeared before Ahab and told *Ahab* that it would not rain or produce dew for years until he said it would. Jezebel was not addressed or even acknowledged as being within earshot of that proclamation. In fact, her name isn't even mentioned in the entire chapter even though it is recorded that he stayed with a widow in her hometown, Zidon. In chapter 18, Elijah sent for *Ahab* and said *Ahab* was responsible for the land being troubled. The Law of Moses, given to all Israelites to be followed, talked about curses they would bring upon themselves for chasing other gods. It also had laws to be followed for judgments and dealing with who would be killed and why. Elijah was obeying the Law, and Jezebel hated him for it because it interrupted her desires. Jezebel believed she had permission to make up her own rules. She hated the Lord and killed the Lord's prophets, but when her prophets were killed according to the Law of the land to which she moved, she hated Elijah even more and called for a hit on him. That day's actions proved Jezebel to be the leader of a useless religion, which made her look like a royal fool.

On a smaller scale (we're talking the average narcissist who is not directly or indirectly in charge of tens of thousands of people), a narcissistic injury would be any exposure to the idea that the Jezebel is wrong. It could be exposing them to be less important than they believe themselves to be, beating them in a competition, getting a better grade or pay raise/job, or anything that does not inflate the narcissist's ego or allow them to get praise and attention. It really could be as minor as looking better in a dress. Because the narcissist is irrational, it can be hard to foresee what could cause narcissistic injury, especially when you never even address the narcissist. However, you can bet on them getting injured and wanting to retaliate when you stand your ground and present irrefutable evidence against what was believed or done. The Jezebel may be enraged, but you may free others from that blindness they suffered by believing her.

Narcissistic rage:

Jezebel vows on her own life that she will make sure Elijah suffers the same fate that her prophets did that day. Elijah has not said one word or sent one message to her, but Jezebel wastes no time sending a messenger with a death threat. She is so outraged by what she has heard and what it means that she only focuses on destroying Elijah. I have no doubt that had Elijah been within reach, she would have grabbed anything she could use as a weapon to strike him dead. I say that based on normal people's reactions when they are fully angered and need to be restrained. At this moment, Jezebel is maniacal.

Narcissists love threats. They will scream at you, curse you and anyone with you, leave vicious voicemails, send hate emails/texts/messages, and possibly try to kill you. Those who tend to have multiple fits of rage are extremely volatile and violent. Sadly, it is usually the ones who cannot defend themselves, children, on the receiving end of these attacks. Typically, narcissists don't rage in front of people outside of their circle or family unit because they want to portray themselves as ideal parents with a superstar child or as a parent who tries her best but has a child that just can't do right for anything. Rages are usually done somewhat secretly and may involve physical abuse such as striking with random objects that leave scars, fighting the children as if they are adults, purposely shaming children in front of others, or anything they can imagine to punish the recipient.

If the intended recipient is too strong to fight or might have them exposed as a criminal, the rage may come in the form of violent actions so the narcissist injures herself and blames the recipient for the injury. They may even threaten to kill themselves to try to get the person to undo what was done and beg for forgiveness.

The reaction is so jarring that the person is caught off guard and usually retreats, wishing they'd never bothered doing anything. This is usually the desired effect because the person is removed from the spotlight and, possibly, humiliated so the narcissist can feel she got revenge.

As horrible as this rage sounds, there is a worse state in which the narcissist will stew.

Posttraumatic Stress Disorder and Depression

According to the National Institute of Mental Health, PTSD can develop after experiencing a highly disturbing event and can result in "fight or flight" responses from the resulting stress even when there is no actual danger present. To be diagnosed, a person must display certain symptoms for an extended period and/or have repeat symptoms. We won't examine all of them, but we can see enough in Elijah to see he is experiencing PTSD, which is often accompanied by depression.

- Flashbacks/tense and on-edge – Elijah just came off a three-year stretch of living off bread and water while on the run from Jezebel, who had initiated an international manhunt to kill him, only to have her swear by her gods that she would kill him in less than 24 hours of finally getting the rain they needed.
- Frightening thoughts – The threat of death and the ability for her to make it happen were very real, as she had prophets of the Lord slain and was enraged about Baal's prophets being slain.
- Fight/flight response – Elijah immediately took flight. The difference is that the Lord did not tell him to go. Elijah's fear took over.

- Avoidance of the person/area associated with traumatic event – Elijah leaves the area to avoid Jezebel and anyone working for her.
- Guilt/negative thoughts about himself/no desire for normal activities – Elijah not only desires not to prophesy anymore, he's given up hope, he's tired of fighting/standing, believes he's useless as a prophet, and asks to die.

Through the rest of the chapter, the Lord is kind and patient with Elijah. He allows him his feelings and helps him work through what he's going through while reminding Elijah that He's still in control. The Lord tells Elijah that there are still 7,000 who stand strong for Him, which means Elijah is not alone even though he felt alone. The Lord anoints three people to carry out His plan, including the next anointed king of Israel and Elisha, a man Elijah would train to be his replacement as prophet. Elisha becomes Elijah's companion. Many of us understand how reassuring and encouraging it is to know there are others who are standing strong under a similar oppression and can support us as we deal with this demonic spirit. Knowing there is someone with whom you can talk openly about what is going on without criticism is very important.

Jezebel on the Prowl

Announcement that Ahab will die:

1 Kings 20

We read the account of a prophet speaking to Ahab about how the Lord will deliver them in war for His sake. After battles, Ahab makes a covenant with the king of Syria instead of killing him. Ahab is told that he will lose his life in place of the life Ahab didn't take of the enemy of Israel. Again, the Lord spoke to Ahab through prophets to tell him exactly what to expect, and Ahab paid it no mind.

1 Kings 21:1-16

1 Kings 21 gives one of the most detailed accounts of Jezebel's demonic actions. It is here that we see the depths to which narcissists will go to obtain their desires.

Summary:

Ahab approached Naboth, the owner of the vineyard near his palace, and asked if he could have the vineyard in exchange for a better vineyard or money. Naboth stated it is part of his inheritance and cannot give it away because the Lord forbid it. Ahab went home and pouted. Jezebel asked him why he was so upset he wouldn't eat. After Ahab told her, she asked him if he was king, which implies that he should have whatever he wants as the ruler of the nation. She told him she'd get the vineyard for Ahab.

Jezebel wrote letters as if she were Ahab and used his seal for authenticity. The letters were sent to nobles, elders, and respected men in the city with instructions to declare a fast with Naboth at a place of honor. Two wicked and ungodly men ("sons of belial") would then stand before them and accuse Naboth of blaspheming God and the king. Naboth would then be taken out and stoned to death. Once this happened, Jezebel announced to Ahab that he could claim the vineyard because Naboth was dead.

<u>Some things we see here:</u>

Discontentment/greed
God complex/delusions of grandeur
Childlike/temper tantrums
They know how far to push you
Revenge for saying "No"
Manipulation/witchcraft
Triangulation
Religious/knows laws of God & lingo
Conspiracy to commit murder
Legal system/Narcissists love to sue
Impersonation/identity theft
Love bombing
The drop/Big scenes
Flying monkeys
Outrageous lies/scapegoat/character assassination
Projection
Theft/steal an inheritance
Destruction of family

Although you are likely to see some of the same behaviors repeat, I want to focus on some that we haven't addressed or that did not stand out as clearly before this chapter. First up: Ahab, the enabler.

<u>Discontentment/Childish behavior</u>

Nothing in this entire chapter would have taken place had Ahab been content with what he already owned or with the answer he had received. Naboth should have been able to say no to the king without retribution.

Naboth means "fruits," which is somewhat symbolic. Naboth's vineyard is coveted. The vineyard was given by God and was to remain in the family from generation to generation. If we jump to the New Testament, we see that Jesus calls Himself the vine and that we are the branches. We are to abide in Him because we cannot bear fruit without Him. The fruit we are to bear is spiritual fruit and laid out in Galatians 5. Naboth might have been willing to sell his plot of land to Ahab had it not been his gift from God, his inheritance, and a sin to sell his inheritance (as Esau had). Naboth may have even thought it would be a good exchange to get a better plot of land. He was actually put in the spot of either telling the king he would not sell the land or disobeying God.

For his faithfulness, he was killed. As with the prophets of the Lord, Jezebel will kill the Lord's followers and not bat an eye. It was a dangerous time to be faithful to the Lord; however, the Lord does not miss what happened and gave divine retribution.

Jezebel's bloody fingerprints are all over this murder, but Ahab still bears blame because it was his temper tantrum that sparked Jezebel to plot. Ahab could have insisted Naboth keep the land and admitted that he was wrong trying to take something from him. Instead, he's angry with Naboth for obeying God and behaves as if he's been slighted about something he's not even allowed to do. However, he knew his wife would concoct a way to get it, and he let her do whatever she wanted to accomplish this.

Narcissists will do things for enablers when they get something from it. In this case, Jezebel gets to pull a power trip, gain more possessions, and attack someone who still obeys the Lord.

<u>Delusions of Grandeur and they know when they're pushing too far</u>

"⁷And Jezebel his wife said unto him, Dost thou now govern the kingdom of Israel? arise, and eat bread, and let thine heart be merry: I will give thee the vineyard of Naboth the Jezreelite." – 1 Kings 21:7

This is subtle, and some may think I'm reading more into the second. However, I have watched people prod others to take action and then stop because the person "shuts down." Instead of pushing Ahab to go get property or to carry out some of the requests/demands she issued in earlier chapters, she tells him to cheer up because she'll handle it.

One of the phrases I've heard from narcissists is to "handle people with kid gloves." This was specifically after saying, "I know how far to push him."

Jezebel practically challenged Ahab by questioning his authority. In Jezebel's mind, no excuse is good enough to deny them what they want – even if it's God's command. To plan any actions beyond this point is to decide they are above the Law and have the right to have what they want, when they want it, at whatever cost. Instead of providing wise wifely counsel, she encourages him to covet and helps him steal even though this would have been a huge problem had anyone taken something from them. Jezebels and those who feel they are above the law act as if they are totally justified in their dealings.

Narcissists never truly grow up. They live in a world of entitlement, expect everyone to bow on command, and behave as a child stuck in a grown person's body throwing temper tantrums. Sometimes the infantile behavior extends to the point of making others parent them, especially their children.

"No" is a trigger word for revenge

Jezebel never even asks why Naboth wouldn't sell the vineyard. (Ahab never says God forbade selling inheritance.) She responded to the fact that someone would tell the king, "no." Truthfully, if people will tell the king he can't have something, it also means the same can be said to her. If his power is limited, then hers is, too. Regardless of what her background is or whether her culture permitted the king whatever he wanted, she's still in someone else's land and has been there long enough to know Israelites are a very peculiar people with their own set of values and rules. Obviously, if she could force another religion onto the people, kill off thousands of the Lord's servants, and scare off Elijah, people are very aware of what this couple is capable of doing. One lone person denying the king, a leader in war, his land was not a minor thing. Naboth had to have a logical reason for denying the sale. Sadly, Jezebel will not accept denial.

Narcissists have strong reactions to being denied anything. It does not matter how small it is or how much sense the reason makes. They become offended and start figuring out how to get the thing from you or something better to make up for it. If they don't verbally badger you into relinquishing the thing, they begin plotting to take it. An example would be when a narcissist offers to drive you somewhere even though you offered to take your car. After the drive, she asks for gas money. You inform her that you didn't expect the ride and already put gas into your car. She cuts you off and tells you not to worry about it because she'll get it another way. The next week she tells you she needs money for car repairs and takes more than it costs to pay the mechanic's bill.

Manipulation/witchcraft

Manipulation is a key tool of the Jezebel. Witchcraft is manipulation. It's not trusting/having faith that God will handle things perfectly and resorting to outside influences to force an outcome because you want to be the god in control. Witchcraft can include the use of spells, magic, enchantment, or taking advantage and trying to use charm and/or looks (ex. makeup that practically creates a new person, seductive clothing, positioning themselves to sexually tease people, etc.) to bewitch people. There isn't much written here "specifically" stating witchcraft, so I'll stick to the actions we should all be able to agree are manipulative.

Jezebel simply isn't Jezebel until she's switching things around for her benefit.

Narcissists live to manipulate people. It's a game of power.

Triangulation or Splitting Friends and Loyalties

Jezebel needs to create a situation that would rid Ahab of Naboth without the deed tracing back to them, while making the death penalty seem justified. This is sometimes referred to as playing puppet master. She sets up Naboth to an honored position. He and his community hear one thing. She sets up false accusers to come in later and then lets the scene play out. It's a "he said, she said" issue where the person who knows everything that is going on will never explain what happened to anyone. Her intention is to introduce chaos to the situation.

Normally, this doesn't get to a heightened stage so quickly. The way this happens in families is narcissistic mother tells golden child (favorite) that scapegoat child (child that gets the most abuse) never comes by to help her and has taken her money. Golden child spends time "consoling" her, telling her how much he cares about her, sends money, and plans to come see her. Golden child thinks scapegoat is selfish and a user. Narcissistic mother tells scapegoat child it's not necessary to come visit her, buy her groceries, and that she doesn't want him to keep spending all his money on her. She then brags about how well golden child is doing at work, how he calls her three times a day to check on her, and that she's going to use her savings to fly him to see her because he gave the last of his money to a relief fund. Scapegoat child now resents brother because he thinks the brother is taking advantage of "poor" mom. Mom pushes one out of the scene to make it look to the other as if scapegoat child doesn't visit when she specifically told him not to come. The brothers become more and more angry at each other and only deal with mom if they don't deal with each other. Mom now has her sons competing for her attention. Both sons are sending her money because they each believe the other isn't contributing, and neither son will discover what happened in reality because they are so angry at each other that they no longer communicate or only communicate about other topics. Narcissistic mom has successfully played her children against each other to her advantage.

At this heightened stage, the narcissist feeds the anger of one or both sides and sits back to watch the sparks fly.

Jezebel's nickname should be "Sue"

According to the Law of Moses, a person could not be sentenced to death unless a minimum of two witnesses attest to the crime. Jezebel does not follow the Law of Moses, but she knows enough to determine what is necessary to get a conviction and then sets it up so that there would be a guilty verdict. The reason for the murder instead of fighting to get people to grant Ahab the land is because she stood no legal chance if she brought the case honestly. Plus, it would put them in an even more unfavorable light with the people because they'd be seen as taking from the little guy. However, if no one is alive to hold the inheritance, then the king would be free to claim the land.

Blasphemy of God was punishable by death. Jezebel, maybe for good measure, had accusations of blasphemy for both God and king. I don't recall seeing a verse that would indicate death is punishment for blaspheming the king. However, speaking against and challenging

God's representatives has ended in deaths (ex. Korah against Moses and Nabal against David), so hearing someone speak against both God and king would likely draw a strong reaction.

Narcissists love a courtroom. They will pursue any opportunity to take property, money, or even dignity away from someone if the reward is worth it. Narcissists will even go so far as to harm themselves in order to win a personal injury lawsuit. This is the person who has the lawyer on speed dial. Not a year goes by that they aren't talking about suing someone for an outrageous sum of money.

Impersonation/Identity Theft

Jezebel signed letters in Ahab's name and used his seal to give the impression that Ahab placed these orders. You could argue that she was just a wife trying to help her husband but using bad judgment, but he was not incapacitated or confused. She didn't fill out forms and pass them to Ahab to read and sign. She took on the role of king and used his identity to start this trial. Again, she's behind the scenes influencing someone to make specific moves or is doing them herself but setting the enabler or her henchmen up to be the responsible party, since it's not done in her name.

Narcissists are pretenders and chameleons. They watch what people around them do and imitate them. Jezebel didn't care about God's law. She knew Israelites cared, so she incorporated it into her plan. She's not in covenant with the people, so she's not interested in a fast. Again, she looked the part. Narcissists are known for forging names, calling companies and pretending to be account owners, opening credit/bills/large accounts using private information, writing themselves letters as if they came from other people, etc. It gives the impression that "somebody said" something and the narcissist is just acting based on what they discovered from this "other" person.

"Love Bombing" – the stage Jezebel tells you how wonderful you are

"[8]So she wrote letters in Ahab's name, and sealed them with his seal, and sent the letters unto the elders and to the nobles that were in his city, dwelling with Naboth. [9]And she wrote in the letters, saying, 'Proclaim a fast, and set Naboth on high among the people:'" – 2 Kings 21:8-9

Jezebel sent out instructions specifically to Naboth's hometown. The people in the city were sure to know Naboth and his character. If he could stand tall and deny the king possession of his inheritance in order to obey the Lord, surely he must be living a Godly life among the people. There would be no question about whether he was fit to lead the people in a fast. To be set "on high" among the people is to be given a chief or head position. A corporate fast is a solemn time, so an assembly for the people would be taken very seriously.

The exact timeframe between the request for Naboth's vineyard and this fast is not known. Let's consider how it looks. Ahab wants property. Naboth denies the king. Ahab goes away upset. A fast is proclaimed by "the king." Naboth is made to sit at the head, an honor few men have had and known only for men who were devoted to the Lord. The request is made by "King Ahab." This appears to send the message that the king is not upset about the property and respects Naboth so much for his dedication to the Lord that he saw it fitting to put him in a place of honor for this religious occasion. No one would have any reason to suspect that the king was anything but satisfied with him. The king actually looks like a great man.

This is the phase where the narcissist shows lots of attention, seems genuinely interested in you and makes you feel special. It doesn't have to be confined only to a romantic relationship. She will talk to you for hours, take you shopping, tell you that you're the best thing since sliced bread, and basically mirror back to you everything he/she thinks you need to hear to let down your guard and be what they need you to be.

Projection

Jezebel wrote that Naboth should be accused of blasphemy against God and king. Naboth did no such thing; however, Jezebel would not honor Yahweh God. She reviled Him and had no problems blaspheming. She saw no problem having someone killed for what she was doing.

Narcissists will blame you for the wrongs they are doing. Some say it's their way of admitting their guilt, but it's not really an admittance if your talk results in someone else receiving shame or punishment for your sins. They accuse people of sleeping around, lying, and stealing when those are the primary things they do regularly. They will pile on the accusations when they're trying to get rid of someone. For instance, a man may accuse you of having multiple affairs when, in reality, he's the one cheating.

Flying Monkeys

Jezebel orders sons of belial ("worthless, lawless" men) to testify against Naboth. Evil people know how to find and attract other evil people. Naboth hadn't done anything and had a reputable character, so she needed people who would carry out her plans.

This reference comes from *The Wizard of Oz*. The witch would devise a scheme against Dorothy and send her flying monkeys to do her bidding. These are generally people who hear her side or what the narcissist wants and start hounding the victim. They tend to have the same effect as a swarm of tiny mosquitoes beside a lake. You know they might be out, but you don't know where they are or when they'll start biting. When they come out, everything about them is irritating – not usually immediately painful – just irksome. This could be done by the narcissist making herself sick so a nurse must call you to guilt you into visiting, having her friend pass on a message, or having several people on hand to immediately come to her side to defend her, praise her, or run an errand.

Smear Campaign/Character Assassination/Egregious Lies/Crowds

Jezebels do some of the most damage when there's an audience. The crowd is necessary to make the smear campaign effective. She was not content to just have Naboth killed off. Jezebel launched a full-on character assassination. To ensure he would get the death penalty, she had two sons of belial (meaning two men without morals) accuse him of blasphemy against God and king. She had Naboth built up to feel appreciated and honored. Any questions or suspicions Naboth might have had about the king being angry at him would be gone because it seemed the king was recognizing him for his Godliness. It may have even come across that Ahab realized he was wrong to ask for what God gave and wanted to show how much he respected Naboth's faithfulness, and he made sure that his entire community was there to witness him leading the fast for the Lord. At the height of this occasion when it was totally unexpected, the lawless men then went before everyone and accused him of blasphemy. It was a shock because it was a testimony of Naboth doing the very opposite of the thing for which he was leading. The Law of Moses required that there be at least two witnesses to pass judgment, and blasphemy wasn't tolerated. It also commanded that no one bring a false accusation/bear false witness against neighbors. Anyone who was found to bear false witness (lie) was to receive the same penalty that would be delivered if the charge had been true. Therefore, the false witnesses would have been stoned if they had been found to be liars.

The accusations were so outrageous that it would be hard to believe that anyone would just make up so serious a lie, especially if they knew the lies would cost them their lives. It's also easier to produce an emotionally charged environment with more people because a mob mentality is likely to form. The law, the witnesses, the penalty, and lack of someone to help defend him as a witness to this nonexistent event led to Naboth being dragged out and stoned to death. Both the character and actual person are assassinated. Jezebel is satisfied.

Narcissists use smear campaigns regularly. Lies are used to discredit you while making them look like generous, kind, and patient people for having the heart to "put up with you for so long." One day you are friends with the narcissist and her friends, and the next day, they want nothing to do with you for no reason. One day, you're confiding in the narcissist and sharing personal details of your life, and the next week, others have heard a completely different account and hate you. Victims have found this tactic used on their own family members as a way for the narcissist to make the relatives allies while everyone alienates the victim.

Lies are not restricted to being about others. Narcissists lie about themselves so often that it is hard to know what is true. When they do lie about themselves, they are usually tearing down someone else in the process to make themselves look better. Some who have been injured repeatedly have stated that "You can tell a narcissist is lying because their lips are moving." In other words, whenever they talk, you can bet there's a lie woven into the conversation. Lies include educational background, family relatives, childhood, any skills, income, parking spaces, living on the sun, etc. They are not above claiming the ridiculous and fully expecting you to believe them. In fact, they will act as if they've been deeply offended and insulted that you refuse to believe they performed their own surgeries because the doctor was on lunch break. Part of the reason for the lie is to penalize you for some perceived wrong, which means they will use different tactics to punish you. This could be as minor as accusing you of stepping on their toes when you passed just to insist you apologize for something you never did.

Steal, Kill, and Destroy:

Jesus said the thief comes to kill, steal, and destroy. Jezebel is the perfect example of what He meant. She stole property by killing the owner and destroyed Naboth's family. Jezebels thrive on demonic, ungodly activity and are walking catastrophes.

Remember that Naboth refused to sell his vineyard because it was his inheritance from the Lord. As they (the 12 tribes of Israel after they were released from Egyptian slavery) were preparing to possess the Promised Land, the Lord explained inheritance would pass from generation to generation. If land was lost due to debt, it would revert to the original family in the Year of Jubilee. If a man died, his sons would inherit the land, then daughters, his brothers, then kinsmen. Basically, in order to get an opportunity to lay claim to Naboth's land, it wasn't enough to kill Naboth. Jezebel had to make sure those with the opportunity to claim the land either didn't or weren't able to claim it.

"[26]Surely I have seen yesterday the blood of Naboth, and the blood of his sons, saith the Lord; and I will requite thee in this plat, saith the Lord…" – 2 Kings 9:26a

Jezebel had Naboth *and* his sons murdered so that she could steal his land. Jezebel destroys families and doesn't care how anyone is affected as long as she gets her stuff.

Narcissists are notorious for driving wedges between people. Where the Lord loves and seeks families to stay intact and seek reconciliation, Jezebel hates and actively seeks to tear them apart. Jezebels will always encourage a divorce. She will be the one in people's ears suggesting adultery, spreading lies, hurrying to file a claim, pushing people into new relationships, using children as pawns, and using every devious opportunity she can to tear a marriage apart. Marriages are a focal point because marriages are a picture of the Lord in covenant with His people. Jesus commanded, "What GOD has joined together let not man put asunder." If the Lord loves it, she hates it. Narcissists will fight especially hard to destroy families if she feels her enabler or victim will put his family first and not give in to her demands, especially if she has trained her victim to financially support her.

God Sentences Ahab and Jezebel to Death

1 Kings 21:17-29

Summary

The Lord instructed Elijah to confront Ahab in Naboth's vineyard. The king calls Elijah his enemy and asks if he's found him. The prophet tells him that because he "sold" himself to do evil in order to obtain the vineyard, dogs would lick his blood in the place where Naboth's was licked. The Lord would end Ahab's dynasty. All the male relatives of Ahab left in Israel would die. Jezebel would die by the wall in Jezreel (Naboth was from Jezreel), and dogs would eat her body. Of all the wickedness of the previous kings and their families to serve idols, none compared to the depths of Ahab's wickedness through Jezebel.

"²⁵But there was none like unto Ahab, which did sell himself to work wickedness in the sight of the Lord, whom Jezebel his wife stirred up."

Ahab heard this, put on garments of mourning, and fasted. The Lord said to Elijah that because Ahab humbled himself, the fall and calamity would happen in his son's lifetime and that Ahab wouldn't have to witness it.

What we see here:

Divine sentencing
Enabler is a willing slave to Jezebel
Jezebel loves chaos
Long-suffering and mercy still offered by the Lord

God's Sentence

Although it wouldn't be carried out immediately, Ahab learns his fate and the fate of his family. Nothing is hidden from God, and He will repay in His time perfectly and justly. Elijah is still only addressing Ahab, but now Elijah has mentioned Jezebel for the first time – to announce where God says she will be killed.

Ahab "sold" himself

The enabler is not off the hook. It doesn't matter if Ahab left the room and refused to hear any plans his wife made. He profited off the death of a man who was murdered due to his wife's scheme. We see that Jezebel is the one in charge as Ahab waits for her plans to fall into place. Jezebel wanted the temples and groves, so Ahab had them built. She wanted Baal worship, so he served her gods. She wanted to kill off the Lord's prophets, so Ahab helped find them so they could be exterminated. The land faced starvation due to the drought because they turned from God, yet she made sure she and her prophets were well fed. Ahab reports to Jezebel, and she ignores the obvious miracles to pursue the man who reminds them of their sins. She decided to snatch Naboth's land, and Ahab allowed her to destroy a whole family to get himself an herb garden. Ahab gets something out of the deals, so he is at fault for allowing them and taking advantage of the situation. He submits to Jezebel's demands, so he is not controlling the kingdom as he should – she is.

Narcissists are attracted to power, prestige, money – anything that will make them feel important and give them the ability to exercise control over others. The bigger the position, the more they want it. It's part of their god complex and desire to be worshiped and the center focus. Enablers do not get to play the innocent role. They may not pull the trigger, but they don't try to prevent the order for the hit either. They will turn over their keys, bank account information, media platform, etc. and will turn a blind eye to what's being done in their name to claim ignorance of the situation. They still have to face consequences of not taking responsibility, and the narcissists will have to deal with the judgment that comes from their actions. Enablers tend to allow narcissists to do whatever they want to avoid hearing their shrieks or complaints, or deal with their rages. Instead of getting rid of the narcissist because she won't sit quietly, the enabler takes small monetary prizes to get a temporary reprieve from the narcissist. Eventually, he learns that by allowing the narcissist her way, he loses everything that might have ever meant anything to him – career, reputation, and his entire family. At the end of the day, the enabler had all the ability to keep the Jezebel from destroying himself and his loved ones, and he didn't.

Jezebel enjoys chaos

Jezebel "stirred up" Ahab. She was instigating. Instead of just letting things lie calmly and peacefully, she "stirred the pot." She stayed in Ahab's ear and continued to influence him to do more and more wickedness until God decided Ahab had to die sooner rather than later.

Nothing is ever calm around the narcissist. The atmosphere is tense. She yells, lies, gossips heavily, is running a smear campaign, participating in triangulation, is trying to figure out how to separate you from your money, is devising a way to break up your marriage, looking for a way to destroy your children, causing a scene at a family function, demanding attention at a funeral, etc. Again, if the Lord loves things like order, peace, and communication, then the Jezebel demands things be as if they were hit by an earthquake, people constantly uneasy or with stomachs in knots, and no one talking or asking questions to others because they might discover the truth.

People stir things to keep them from being settled or to get things so mixed up that you can't tell what's what. This is the uneasy feeling people have knowing the narcissist will attempt to provoke someone to fight or will create drama on purpose. Sometimes this comes in the form circular arguments where the narcissist keeps changing topics and complaints to keep you off balance. The narcissist causes people to always have their guards up because she likes watching people trying to defend themselves against lies, look hurt because of her accusations, or end relationships. Her motives could be as small as just wanting to make you give in to her choice of restaurant, but everything is done for her control and to get her desires.

God is still merciful

When Ahab acknowledged his wickedness by tearing his clothes, fasting, and wearing sackcloth, the Lord saw. No words are recorded, but the Lord saw his actions and chose to postpone the timing of when the line would be cut off and Jezebel killed. Due to his actions in the war of the previous chapter of making a covenant with enemy king Benhadad, Ahab was told he would die. For permitting the murder of an innocent man and his sons, Ahab, his sons, and Jezebel would lose their lives and dynasty in Israel. However, Ahab showed some sign of acknowledging his wrong, so he would be spared watching his family die in front of his eyes.

The Bible says that the Lord is long-suffering and not willing that any should perish (eternally). He seeks those who seek Him. He is willing to welcome those who come to Him and believe on Him. Forgiveness does not erase consequences, but it is available with repentance. I don't think Ahab's behavior qualifies as repentant, but it does show that he recognized that he was wrong. We haven't seen that since we were introduced to him in chapter 16.

Ahab's Final Warning from God

1 Kings 22

Summary

The king of Judah (Jehoshaphat) came to the king of Israel (Ahab), and Ahab asked for support to take Ramothgilead from Syria. Jehoshaphat was a Godly king. After Jehoshaphat agreed to go to battle with Ahab, Jehoshaphat asked for a prophet to advise them according to the way of the Lord. Micaiah was the only one who would speak the Lord's words even when they were hard to hear. About 400 prophets spoke in the Lord's name that the kings would be victorious. Micaiah stated the Lord allowed a lying spirit to seduce the prophets to persuade Ahab to go into battle. If the kings went to battle, the troops would return defeated because Ahab would be killed.

Ahab hated Micaiah because of the things he would tell the king, and Ahab refused to listen. Ahab had Micaiah imprisoned to be fed with bread and water until his return. Micaiah gave a final warning to everyone and stated if Ahab returned, the Lord didn't speak through Micaiah (the test of a true prophet).

Jehoshaphat wore his kingly robes, and Ahab changed clothes to disguise himself. The enemy, king of Syria, commanded his captains to target the king of Israel, Ahab. During the fight, they captured Jehoshaphat but turned him loose when they realized he was not their target. By "random" Divine chance, some soldier shot into the air and struck Ahab. The king ordered the chariot driver to leave the battle area. The battle continued, Ahab watched, and he died in the chariot by evening. The troops were sent home. The chariot was washed out, and the dogs licked his blood from where it spilled as God had foretold.

Ahaziah, Ahab's son, became king over Israel during Jehoshaphat's seventeenth year of ruling over Judah.

"⁵¹Ahaziah the son of Ahab began to reign over Israel in Samaria the seventeenth year of Jehoshaphat king of Judah, and reigned two years over Israel. ⁵²And he did evil in the sight of the Lord, and walked in the way of his father, **and in the way of his mother**, and in the way of Jeroboam the son of Nebat, who made Israel to sin: ⁵³For he served Baal, and worshipped him, and provoked to anger the Lord God of Israel, according to all that his father had done." – 1 Kings 22:51-53

What we see here:

God's Word will come to pass
False prophets/flatterers
Hardened heart
Jezebel's influence continues

God's judgment carried out

Ahab attempted to avoid being killed by disguising himself. A "random" soldier shot an arrow and "just happened" to deliver a fatal blow to the king. What the Lord said will come to pass.

People who willingly participate in evil will receive a righteous judgment somehow one way or another.

False Prophets

The showdown at Mt. Carmel resulted in the deaths of the prophets of Baal. Even though some years have passed and Baal worship is still heavy, Jezebel has changed her tactics somewhat. It does not take 400+ prophets to deliver God's Word to one man, as we saw when Elijah spoke and when Micaiah spoke. These prophets are playing the role of Godly spiritual counsel while lying in His name. Jehoshaphat, a Godly king, discerned immediately that none of the king's prophets spoke for the Lord.

"⁶Then the king of Israel gathered the prophets together, about four hundred men, and said unto them, Shall I go against Ramothgilead to battle, or shall I forbear? And they said, Go up; for the Lord shall deliver it into the hand of the king. ⁷And Jehoshaphat said, Is there not here a prophet of the Lord besides, that we might enquire of him? ⁸And the king of Israel said unto Jehoshaphat, There is yet one man,

Micaiah the son of Imlah, by whom we may enquire of the Lord: but I hate him; for he doth not prophesy good concerning me, but evil. And Jehoshaphat said, Let not the king say so." – 1 Kings 22:6-8

We will see this again. Jezebel has mixed the Godly with the profane. From earlier accounts, we know Jezebel would not allow so many people of the Lord nearby on purpose. Having the prophets in service to the king gives the illusion of following the Lord or having faith in Him when the reality is that they only appear to follow God when it suits their purpose. (We see this display from people who teach a false gospel.) They have still surrounded themselves with false religion and people who are against the Lord while despising those who speak for the Lord. Another thing to recognize is that these prophets are flatterers. They speak in exaggerated lies as if the narcissist were speaking.

"[11]And Zedekiah the son of Chenaanah made him horns of iron: and he said, Thus saith the Lord, With these shalt thou push the Syrians, until thou have consumed them." – 1 Kings 22:11

Zedekiah didn't just lie. He made props to help illustrate the thing that would not happen. It wasn't enough to say they'd win big and be victorious. His description has the kings practically annihilating the Syrians, and he decides to take a stab at theater acting by displaying how they'd defeat the army. He then struck Micaiah for calling him on his lie.

We recognize this as "ear-tickling" sermons and prophecies. Today's show-boating title grabbers love to proclaim your health and wealth or yell that this is your year because "God said so." They have no Scripture to back up what they say, or they use passages and twist them to mean something they don't. There are many people teaching a false gospel and sharing ungodly messages disguised as revelations from God.

Narcissists surround themselves with people who will flatter them while shunning those who do not. They would rather be told a lie about how magnificent they are and how great their accomplishments will be than have someone honestly tell them they don't stand a chance at something. When we look at Zedekiah, think about what he said, the lengths he went to demonstrate his point, and the fact that he hit Micaiah in the face for speaking the truth about the king's fate, we can see that the narcissist's home and counsel will be comprised of sycophants who will fight to protect the lies they tell for the narcissist.

Hard-heartedness

Although the Lord permitted a lying spirit into the mouths of the prophets, he also permitted Ahab one final chance to heed the Word of the Lord. Micaiah was known to speak what the Lord said, which is why Ahab did not want to hear from him. Jehoshaphat insisted. Ahab knew…absolutely knew…that Micaiah spoke what God said and heard the prophet issue a warning to all of Israel within hearing distance of his voice. That's why he took the time to change clothes and try to fight undercover. Yet Ahab had allowed himself to become so far gone in following Jezebel that he refused to listen to the one man he knew would tell the truth and, in essence, chose not to save his life. Ahab was an Israelite and knew the history. He'd talked to Elijah on several occasions. He had seen fire come down from the sky with his own two eyes. He humbled himself when Elijah confronted him about stealing Naboth's land even though it would have been nearly impossible to trace the murder back to himself and only possible if God knew it. After all the problems Ahab had caused and after having a chance to witness the Lord's miracles, he knew when a true prophet was speaking. Yet he chose not to listen, and his pride cost him his life.

The Lord has provided people a way of life. Even those who adamantly hate Him are given an opportunity to choose to listen to Him. He has offered people to teach His Word, a Book that holds the Scriptures, and the Promised Redeemer for salvation. The same way Ahab can't say he was never given warning of how to avoid destruction is the same way we can't claim we were never given the opportunity to learn about the Gospel. Like Ahab, we are given full disclosure of the outcome of our choices for salvation. If we are destroyed, it's not because we weren't warned. It's because we chose to move forward with our own plans, to our own peril.

Jezebel is still influencing the king

63

It is highly unusual to mention following a mother's ways unless the Bible mentions her teaching or guiding a young child. Ahaziah was a grown man when he took the throne. He continued to serve and worship Baal and continued as Ahab had done. Ahab followed and answered to Jezebel. If Ahaziah followed Ahab's steps, then he followed and answered to Jezebel also.

This is the relationship we see when narcissistic women have a son-husband. She tells him what to do and rules through him because she feels her son should obey her while she has the privilege of living well as he supports and provides for her as her husband would. Women with son-husbands who are not married typically won't marry, so they continue to give the impression that the only one who can care for them is the son. People who see this dynamic usually hear the narcissistic mother say things that indicate she believes she owns him, that he owes his allegiance to her, she's the most important person in his life, he'll listen to her above everyone else, he'll always take care of her, etc. Jezebel was so involved in Ahaziah's life that she got a place of mention among the ways of the fathers' paths, and all three of them were ungodly, with Jezebel being the reason Ahab is considered the most wicked king of all of Israel's kings.

Jezebel's Second Son Begins to Reign/Elijah Goes to Heaven

2 Kings 1

Summary

Moab, a people conquered decades prior, rebelled and was another sign that Israel was losing its hold over territories. King Ahaziah fell through his lattice and lay severely injured. He sent messengers to go ask Baal/Baalzebub, in another country, if he'd recover. The Lord sent an angel to tell Elijah to meet the messengers to report back that since Ahaziah would seek out another god, he would die in his bed. Ahaziah recognized the prophet was Elijah by the description given by his messengers.

The king then ordered a captain and fifty men to order Elijah to come to Ahaziah. The captain addressed him, and Elijah called down fire from Heaven that killed the men. Ahaziah sent a second captain with a second fifty to order him to come quickly. Elijah called down fire from Heaven again. When the third captain went with his fifty, he humbled himself and asked Elijah to return with them. The angel told him to go and not worry.

Elijah repeated his message to Ahaziah, and the king later died. Jehoram, Ahaziah's brother, became king because Ahaziah had no sons.

What we see here:

Ungodly parental influence

Ahaziah was so familiar with Elijah, or his legacy, that he recognized him by description. By the time he reached this point of death, he had had plenty of time to show his stripes and repent of his ways. Instead of seeking answers from the Lord, he sought advice from an idol. When he hears word from the Lord, he sends a small army to arrest Elijah. By the third time, he hasn't understood that his tactics don't cause God to move for him. Like his parents, he knows the history, he knows Elijah speaks the truth, he hears words sent to him from the prophet of God and refuses to change any of his ways even on his deathbed.

The choices we make and the things we teach our children can influence them to improve their lives or walk them to their graves. This is not really a concern for narcissists. It's as if their thinking is, "I have/can have more children." Business as usual.

2 Kings 2

Elijah the prophet is taken to Heaven in a fiery chariot, and Elisha steps into his place as prophet.

2 Kings 3

Summary

"¹Now Jehoram the son of Ahab began to reign over Israel in Samaria the eighteenth year of Jehoshaphat king of Judah, and reigned twelve years. ²And he wrought evil in the sight of the Lord; but not like his father, and like his mother: for he put away the image of Baal that his father had made. ³Nevertheless he cleaved unto the sins of Jeroboam the son of Nebat, which made Israel to sin; he departed not therefrom." – 2 Kings 3:1-3

Jehoram put away the Baal images for worship but kept the false worship initiated by Jeroboam (first king of the Northern Kingdom), who built a golden calf in a temple.

Moab stopped paying tribute to Israel. King Jehoram (Israel) asked King Jehoshaphat (Judah) to join him in battle against Moab. The king of Edom joined them. After a seven-day journey with no water, Jehoram accused God of leading them to destruction and into their enemy's hands. Jehoshaphat asked about a prophet of God. Elisha was sought.

"¹³And Elisha said unto the king of Israel, What have I to do with thee? get thee to the prophets of thy father, **and to the prophets of thy mother**. And the king of Israel said unto him, Nay: for the Lord hath called these three kings together, to deliver them into the hand of Moab. ¹⁴And Elisha said, As the Lord of hosts liveth, before whom

I stand, surely, were it not that I regard the presence of Jehoshaphat the king of Judah, I would not look toward thee, nor see thee." – 2 Kings 2:13-14

Elisha only deals with them for Jehoshaphat's sake because the king of Judah strives to follow the Lord. He instructs them to build ditches for water and told them God would give them victory. It never rained, but the ditches filled with water for all men and animals to drink. When Moabites saw it the next day, they saw what looked like blood and assumed the kings were dead. When they advanced, the kings and armies beat them back, took spoils, and the Moabite king was so worried that he sacrificed his successor son to his god. The Israelites were filled with indignation, stopped fighting, and went home.

What we see here:

Reference to mother Jezebel again
Ungodly king trying to get in good with Godly king

Jezebel is still quietly in the picture

Twice in this chapter, we see Jehoram is still following his mother's ways. It is unusual to make note of a man following after his mother, especially twice in the same chapter. The reference shows us the ungodly influence actively affecting this king, especially when he tells Elisha that God got those three kings together to be defeated.

Religious mix

It appears that Jehoram only deals with people of God when it benefits him. Instead of pushing the Baal worship, they have put away the visible images but are still not committed to God, as is evident by Elisha addressing the fact that he is interested in the words of a prophet of a God he doesn't serve. It also appears that he is hoping that he'll get blessed by hanging out with God's people; he wants the good things of God without God. The three kings all witness the miracle, but Jehoshaphat is the only one we know to acknowledge the One Who did it.

Elisha's Miracles and the Mercy of God to His Enemies

2 Kings 4–8

These are fast-paced chapters with Elisha performing several miracles of God. Some include:

Chapter 4 – A Shunammite woman feeds Elisha and provides him a spare room since she recognizes he is a prophet of the Lord. He discovers she has no child, prays for the Lord to give her and her husband (elderly) a child, and she has a son. A few years pass, and the child dies. The Shunammite woman seeks Elisha with faith that he will hear her. Elisha prays, and God brings the child back to life.

Chapter 5 – Naaman, captain of the Syrian army (enemy), has leprosy. His servant tells him of Elisha. Naaman seeks him out, is instructed to dip seven times in the Jordan River, discusses it, follows instructions, and is cured.

Chapter 6 – The king of Syria brought war to Israel. Every time he discussed his battle plans among his leaders, Elisha would hear from the Lord to tell King Jehoram their attack strategies and how to win. The king of Syria was told there was no spy among them but Elisha knew. The king sent an army of men to bring Elisha to him. When they arrived, an angel struck them with blindness. Elisha guided them directly to the capital of Israel, Samaria. King Jehoram asked if they should be killed, but Elisha stated no, gave them something to eat and drink, and let them return to their king to say what's been done. After a time, Benhadad, king of Syria, encamped around the city to starve the inhabitants into giving up. Jehoram saw the people of his city so starved they ate their children. He put on sackcloth. He then swore by God that Elisha would be dead by the end of the day.

"[31]Then he said, God do so and more also to me, if the head of Elisha the son of Shaphat shall stand on him this day. [32]But Elisha sat in his house, and the elders sat with him; and the king sent a man from before him: but ere the messenger came to him, he said to the elders, See ye how this son of a murderer hath sent to take away mine head? look, when the messenger cometh, shut the door, and hold him fast at the door: is not the sound of his master's feet behind him?" – 2 Kings 6:31-32

Chapter 7 – Elisha tells them that by the next day, food would be so plenteous, it would be cheap, but the king's man who questioned it wouldn't live to taste it. The king doubted and sent a group to check it out to find out it was true. The Syrians had fled in fear and left their supply.

Chapter 8:1-15 – Elisha had told the Shunammite woman and her son to leave due to a famine that would come and last seven years. When she returned to request her property, the former servant of Elisha was telling the king about the miracles and announced the woman in front of them was the mother of the child who had died and been given life again. King Benhadad of Syria fell deathly ill and sent for word from Elisha to find out if he would recover. The messenger, Hazael, was told he could recover but would die, as God had already appointed Hazael to be the king of Syria (one of the three appointments told to Elijah after his run from Jezebel). Hazael would be a ruthless, heartless, and murderous king. The next day, Hazael smothered Benhadad until he died.

What we see here:

Elisha is doing similar miracles as Elijah. He had a double portion of blessing and did twice as many even to the point that the famine lasted twice as long as the drought (three and a half years usually just stated as three years of no rain or dew).

Non-covenant people who do not have God's laws know there is a true God. The Lord seeks to bless them for their belief, repentance, and faith in Him, too. Even Israel's enemy commander was cured. He trusted in the faith of his servant who believed Elisha spoke for God and humbled himself enough to do as God instructed.

Jehoram has impressionable interactions with Elisha, much like his parents with Elijah, and has seen miracles with his own eyes. However, he still threatens to kill the man of God with the language Jezebel used threatened Elijah. This time, he swore by the Lord instead of by "the gods." He is around Godly people, but he never lets anything penetrate his heart.

Introducing Athaliah: The Two-fold Child of Jezebel Hell

2 Kings 8:16-29

This section will go a bit quickly because it gives an overview of several years. It is here because it is the next section of 2 Kings as we move through the life of Jezebel. This is the section of time where we see Jezebel's poison infiltrate another kingdom. The passages in 2 Kings give us more details about what happens in Israel while the parallel passages in 2 Chronicles will give us more details about what happens in Judah. We will reference both as we continue in order to give a fuller picture of how Jezebel damaged the second and third generations.

Honestly, this is the point in my study where I had to create a chart (the "cheat sheet" included earlier) to make sure I could keep the names and kingdoms straight. For Bible students and those who want to read these sections, the passages are 2 Kings 8:16-29 and 2 Chronicles 22:5-6. The Books of the Kings are written with the perspective of the rulers and families (ex. lineages). The Books of the Chronicles are written from a theological perspective or how things are seen in view of how they line up with God (ex. preserving the lives of the ancestors of Christ).

Points to help minimize confusion:

- Athaliah is Jezebel's daughter and has married Jehoram of Judah.
- Jehoram of Judah is the brother-in-law of Jehoram of Israel.
- Jehoshaphat let Jehoram co-reign with him until he died. When Jehoram died, his son, Ahaziah reigned (Grandfather, son, grandson).
- Jehoram of Judah is the son-in-law of Ahab and Jezebel and followed in their footsteps instead of the footsteps of his own father.

- At the end of this chapter, Jezebel's son is ruling in Israel, and her grandson is ruling in Judah under the guidance of her daughter, Athaliah.

Summary

We have two Jehorams/Jorams at this time who are both kings of their territories. Jehoram of Israel, son of Ahab was already ruling. Jehoram of Judah, son of Godly Jehoshaphat, reigned in the south. He co-ruled with his father and continued ruling after Jehoshaphat's death. Even though his father was Godly, the alliance/friendship that Jehoshaphat had allowed without consulting God led to his son marrying Ahab's (and Jezebel's) daughter and their falling away from the Lord to do what Ahab's family did, which means the Jehorams are now family by marriage. The Lord's promise to David to give him a blood descendent for the throne prevented God from destroying the lineage in Judah.

The Bible makes it clear that Jehoram of Judah followed in the way of his father-in-law instead of his father and that Athaliah was very influential in the lives of her husband and her son. At the end of the chapter, we see King Ahaziah (Judah) joins with King Jehoram (Israel) to fight against King Hazael (Syria). Jehoram returns to Israel wounded, and Ahaziah goes to visit his Uncle Jehoram.

What we see here:

Quick update
Jezebel's influence has permeated another kingdom
Setting the stage for fall of the house of Ahab

Update

This chapter gives a brief summary of several years. In Judah, Jehoshaphat dies, and Jehoram becomes king. Jehoram dies, and Ahaziah becomes king.

Jezebels birth more Jezebels

The second two kings, Jehoram and Ahaziah of Judah, were not young when they took the throne. They had time to learn and see the lessons from Jehoshaphat. Athaliah carries on the traditions her mother taught her. She is the second Jezebel. Her legacy at this point

71

is to give wicked counsel. Her family is noted as having given wicked counsel. They taught Jehoram to follow their practices and ended up being the death of him.

Again, the Bible makes several mentions about Ahaziah's mother, her influence, and how everything attached to the house of Ahab is worth wiping out due to their sin. We see a repeat of the marriage of Ahab and Jezebel here. Ahab and Jezebel's marriage was a political move. With it came Jezebel's gods from her country into her new country. Jehoram of Judah married Athaliah of Israel, daughter of Ahab, to bring the Northern and Southern Kingdoms closer in what appears to be a political power move and alliance. She also brings her customs, rituals, and false religion to her new land.

Narcissists tend to make, or attempt to make, clones of themselves. A narcissistic mother may influence her daughter or a girl she's taken on as a daughter to be another version of herself. They will look like best friends separated by a generation. The second will have the same nasty attitude/rude mouth, behave similarly, and will continue to look to the original Jezebel for advice/wicked counsel.

Preparing for the Fall of Ahab's House

When Elijah went on the run from Jezebel, God told him three people were chosen as replacements. Elisha replaced Elijah. Hazael replaced King Benhadad in Syria, and the king to replace Ahab's lineage is about to be anointed.

Second-Generation Jezebel: The King Murders His Brothers

2 Chronicles 21

1 & 2 Samuel and 1 & 2 Kings are considered books of the kings and tell what's going on regarding their lineage, activity, and reign. 1 & 2 Chronicles give us more information about Israel's national history told from a perspective that focuses more on God. To get a better understanding of Jehoram of Judah's rapid decline and the depth of his sin influenced by Jezebel across the border, we need to examine a parallel passage of Scripture that will fill us in on what happened between the time he co-reigned with his father to the time his son took over upon his death.

Summary

Before Jehoshaphat died, he appointed his oldest son, Jehoram, to reign in his place. To his other sons, he gave jewels, monetary gifts, and land. However, when Jehoshaphat died, Jehoram "strengthened himself" and killed all his brothers. He spent his time in power following Ahab's example because he married Ahab and Jezebel's daughter, Athaliah. But God wouldn't wipe out Jehoram and all his family because of the promise made to David. Jehoram was a blood descendant.

Edomites revolted under his rule, and that caused perpetual strife between the nations.

"¹¹Moreover he made high places in the mountains of Judah and caused the inhabitants of Jerusalem to commit fornication, and **compelled** Judah thereto." – 2 Chron 21:11

Elijah sent a message to the king (remember this is a parallel passage, so this message was sent before Elisha began his ministry as a prophet), which stood out since he was living in the Northern Kingdom. The Lord said that Jehoram wasn't following the steps of his Godly predecessors, including his father, and made Judah sin in worshiping idols. Jehoram was following his father-in-law, Ahab, and leading Judah into the whoredoms of Ahab's family ways. He had also killed all his brothers.

The punishment from the Lord would be a plague upon his people. His wives and sons were taken by his enemies except his youngest, Jehoahaz/Ahaziah. The Lord struck the king with an incurable disease in his bowels that would affect him for two years, get progressively worse, and ultimately kill him when they fell out. No one mourned his passing.

What we see here:

Jezebel's influence is immediate and forceful
Paranoia/Eliminate competition/Bloodthirsty
Enabling her destroyed the enabler – not Jezebel

Paranoid/Murdered brothers/bloodthirsty

Jehoshaphat had ensured everyone heard the law and that the Law of God was enforced during his reign. When Jehoram finally had full control over the kingdom after his father passed, he murdered his brothers. Since Jehoshaphat had been trying to please the Lord and had taught his family and country the same, it is obvious that this murderous spirit came from Athaliah's influence – Jezebel II. There was no need to kill his brothers because:

1. It had already been established that he would be king after Jehoshaphat because he was appointed to co-reign while the previous king was alive.
2. Jehoram was the oldest son, and the oldest sons are usually expected to continue in their father's business (in this case, ruling a kingdom) unless there were extenuating circumstances.
3. Judah was the kingdom carrying the bloodline of royalty and the genealogy of the Promised Seed for the entire world. No one knew when He would be born, so it would have been beyond detrimental and irreparable to kill off a possible ancestor to Him. Only Israel, the Northern Kingdom, changed dynasties. Judah understood her kings were appointed by God.

The spirit of hatred, divisiveness, and lust for power through bloodshed came from Jezebel's influence but is now elevated to killing off siblings. There is no indication that any of the brothers were jealous or were plotting to take the throne. This was an unnecessary move. Remember, Jezebel is a murderer at heart. She hates and does not love.

Narcissists see everyone as competition. They look at you as if you want to take their position or perceived power and will seek to eliminate any perceived threats even when you have no intention of doing anything other than living your normal life. They want to be the only option for any spot. Often, this is understood as narcissists acting out their own paranoid ideas. They believe others would behave as they would, so they seek to get rid of anyone they believe is a threat.

<u>Influence is strong and pervasive</u>

Jehoshaphat's saying, "I am as thou art" and trying to make an alliance with Ahab brought in much unforeseen trouble. Athaliah came into their lives having grown up under Ahab and Jezebel. Much like Jezebel knowing the ways of Baal, Athaliah followed those beliefs, knew Israel's history, and was now spreading their ways into Judah since she was of the Northern Kingdom but living as queen in the Southern Kingdom. Jezebel's dirty fingers are all over the entire Israelite people (all 12 tribes).

Jehoram made high places for the gods of Athaliah, led Jerusalem (capital city and location for temple worship to the Lord) into fornication (likely to primarily mean idolatry although we remember that Baal worship also involved sexual activity), and "compelled" Judah to follow. He was actively involved in leading his kingdom away from the Lord. To have a Godly father to have the influence and recognition for centuries afterward for his walk with the Lord, Jehoram had to work extra hard to go so far in the opposite direction in a mere eight years to not even have people mourn his demise. The words she said to her husband had a significant enough impact on him to make him completely turn his back on God – the same God Who was still performing miracles in his lifetime. People in the

75

Southern Kingdom were well aware of Elijah's miracles. The fact that Elijah had been told by the Lord to send word to Judah was big. Prophets of Judah had been sent to Jehoshaphat telling him of the Lord's displeasure at his alliance with Ahab or Ahab's first ruling son, Ahaziah. Jehoram was not blinded. He aligned himself fully to what God hated and pushed Judah to worship idols.

Narcissists love to corrupt. They want to undo good things and Godly people. If taking people of God out of the picture is too complicated or backfires, such as the killing of the Lord's prophets and the battle of the gods, they seek to change people's beliefs. This is usually most effective by mixing beliefs and encouraging the tolerance of their gods. The Bible states two cannot walk together unless they be agreed. One will influence the other to go in his direction. You cannot join yourself to someone who hates God and think you will still be able to walk in His ways as you once did. Typically, to keep the peace, the Godly one will make the compromise. This is usually one of the first ways victims feel they are "losing themselves" because they are always yielding to the whims and will of the narcissist.

Narcissists want their way. Notice Jehoram compelled the nation of Judah to follow other gods – likely Baal and Asherah. Just as Jezebel did with Ahab, Athaliah worked through Jehoram to get her high places to worship her gods while expecting the country to which she moved to accommodate and follow her. Narcissists expect total compliance, funding for their projects, and for everyone to change their ways of living or doing things to do it the narcissist's way. It is also likely that murdering the brothers was to prevent anyone close to the king and his status from appealing to his conscience to do what is right by God. If the people or God would have demanded him step down or for them to be stoned for idolatry, a brother could still rule because he carried the royal bloodline. Killing off other potential kings ensured Athaliah's husband would stay in power.

Enablers bring their own destruction:

Just as Ahab was judged by God for allowing Jezebel to have her way, Jehoram was judged by God for allowing Athaliah to have her way. Both kings went out of their way to make it possible and simple for their wives to defy God. Both pushed for their kingdoms to worship the gods of their wives. Both participated in the senseless slaughter of innocent people. The Jezebels prompted their husbands, and the husbands were eventually sentenced to death as judgments for their crimes. Both husbands received their sentences from Elijah the prophet, and both husbands' families would be affected/destroyed because they refused to deny the Jezebels' demands.

As we've mentioned previously, enablers are not exempt from punishment. They are very much aware of how damaging narcissists are. To avoid short-term discomfort, such as hearing them nag, they go along with the narcissists' plans to their own peril. They are responsible for their actions and their participation regardless of how direct or indirect it is. They are still required to fulfill the obligations of their positions. The same way a soldier can't just walk away from his post as watchman/guard and blame the enemy for killing the men in his unit while they slept is the same way the enabler is held accountable. The narcissist needs the enabler in order to inflict the damage she does because he is the one with the access to what the narcissist wants! Most damage to victims will be greatly minimized when the enabler stops entertaining the narcissist by giving her his ear to poison his thoughts.

A New King in Israel: Judgment Comes to the House of Ahab

2 Kings 9:1-29

Parallel passage – 2 Chronicles 22:5-9

Summary

Elisha instructs one of the young men who learned from him to anoint Jehu, an army captain, king of Israel. The young man is instructed to go to Ramothgilead, speak to Jehu privately, anoint him, inform him that God has appointed him king over Israel, and tell him that he is tasked with killing Ahab's dynasty and Jezebel. This is judgment for the Lord's servants who were slain under Ahab through Jezebel. Her body would be eaten by dogs. After completing the task, the servant bolted out of the camp.

After the men asked Jehu what happened and learned of his anointing, they blew trumpets and proclaimed him king. The men got in their chariots and rode furiously to Jezreel to go after Jehoram, King of Israel, who was recovering from wounds. (Both men couldn't be king.) A watchman spotted Jehu coming, so Jehoram sent a messenger to ask him about how things were going. When that messenger was spotted not returning, another was sent. After he didn't return, King Jehoram and King Ahaziah, of Judah and nephew of King Jehoram, (remember that he had gone to visit when he learned his uncle was injured) got in their chariots to meet Jehu – in Naboth's land.

"²²And it came to pass, when Joram saw Jehu, that he said, Is it peace, Jehu? And he answered, What peace, so long as the whoredoms of thy mother Jezebel and her witchcrafts are so many? ²³And Joram turned his hands, and fled, and said to Ahaziah, There is treachery, O Ahaziah. ²⁴And Jehu drew a bow with his full strength and smote Jehoram between his arms, and the arrow went out at his heart, and he sunk down in his chariot." – 2 Kings 9:22-24

Jehu shot an arrow that went through Jehoram. His body was tossed into Naboth's field in fulfilled prophecy. They pursued Ahaziah, who had chosen to follow his grandfather's ways, and killed him when they found him hiding in Samaria, the capital of the Northern Kingdom. Ahaziah's body was sent back and buried in Jerusalem with other previous kings of Judah.

At the end of this passage, the reigning kings of Israel and Judah were killed.

What we see here:

Jezebel's enablers are taken out:

According to the word of Elijah, Ahab and his male descendants in Israel would be killed. His son's body was tossed into Naboth's field as a Divine repayment and reminder for Ahab's (through the plot of Jezebel) murdering Naboth for his vineyard. Ahaziah of Israel is the grandson of Ahab and was killed because he was in the area and because of his participation in continuing the evils of Jezebel through his mother, Athaliah.

While we may not see justice for those who know, encourage, participate in, or turn a blind eye to the evils done by narcissists, they will fall and fall hard in some manner. The Lord doesn't miss what is done. It also serves as a warning to the enablers, especially if they are hoping to outlive the narcissist for some prize like money from a will. Original Jezebel, at this point, has influenced and lived through the death of five (5) kings who were directly influenced to give in to her demands:

1. Ahab – husband, killed by an arrow during a battle after a prophet warned him not to go
2. Ahaziah – son, died on his bed of injury after he sought counsel from an idol
3. Jehoram – son, killed by Jehu who was anointed to wipe out the dynasty
4. Jehoram – son-in-law, died after suffering two years of a bowel disease
5. Ahaziah – grandson, killed by Jehu who was anointed to wipe out the dynasty

All of these deaths were foretold by Elijah, and Ahab was the only one recorded as ever having shown the slightest bit of remorse or humility, which is how his fate was altered slightly after wearing sackcloth and ashes. He did not have to watch the dynasty topple before his eyes. Sadly, even though Jezebel and Athaliah did the persuading, it was the permissiveness and enforcement of the enablers that caused so many victims to be injured or killed.

Jezebel Is Overthrown... Literally

2 Kings 9:30-39

"³⁰And when Jehu was come to Jezreel, Jezebel heard of it; and she painted her face, and tired her head, and looked out at a window. ³¹And as Jehu entered in at the gate, she said, Had Zimri peace, who slew his master? ³²And he lifted up his face to the window, and said, Who is on my side? who? And there looked out to him two or three eunuchs. ³³And he said, Throw her down. So they threw her down: and some of her blood was sprinkled on the wall, and on the horses: and he trode her under foot." – 2 Kings 9:30-33

Immediately after driving his chariot over Jezebel's body, Jehu went inside to eat. He gave it some thought and then sent men to retrieve her body to bury her since she had been royalty. However, all that remained were her skull, hands, and feet because the dogs had eaten her body according to the Word of the Lord given by Elijah to Ahab when he delivered sentencing in Naboth's vineyard.

What we see here:

Jezebel is a witch
Jezebel is a whore/seductress
Intimidation tactics
No contact
Do not engage Jezebel
Jezebel is unrepentant
Jezebel must be stopped
People want Jezebel out of their lives

Jezebel is a witch

Jezebel has dedicated her entire life to the worship of Baal and has spent all her effort calling on demonic entities to give her what she wants. She is manipulative, relies on her charm/words/flattery to influence people, and is reliant on everything God is against to get her way.

The narcissist's main tool of witchcraft is manipulation. However, some narcissists will actively practice a form of witchcraft, spellcasting, or voodoo to try to gain more power over their victims. (Jehu had said she had done much witchcraft.) Some actually admit their practices while continuing to look for items of yours and ways to get into your head or to wreak havoc in your life. Those who seek to twist God's Word for their own gain are practicing also.

"20Notwithstanding I have a few things against thee, because thou sufferest that woman Jezebel, which calleth herself a prophetess, to teach and to seduce my servants to commit fornication, and to eat things sacrificed unto idols." – Revelation 2:20

In this letter from Jesus to the Church at Thyatira, we see Jezebel (a person acting in her spirit – a narcissist) has elevated herself to hold a prominent position inside the church in order to mislead them. There are people who will use a church platform in order to get a power rush there. We can see some Jezebels on TV today. These narcissists speak as if they are saying something of God, yet the purpose is to cause people to look to them and walk away from God (remember, she hates all righteous things).

Jezebel is a whore and sexual pervert:

"22And it came to pass, when Joram saw Jehu, that he said, Is it peace, Jehu? And he answered, What peace, so long as the **whoredoms** of thy mother Jezebel and her witchcrafts are **so many**?" – 2 Kings 9:22

"30And when Jehu was come to Jezreel, Jezebel heard of it; and she painted her face, and tired her head, and looked out at a window." – 2 Kings 9:30

Revelation 2:20-22 talks of her seducing people who will commit fornication and adultery (spiritual and/or physical) with her and then cast into her bed to be destroyed with her.

Baal worship requires sexual acts as part of the practice, particularly to encourage their god to have sex and bring them blessings.

Jezebel did not miss a beat. She is told Jehu is coming to town to claim the throne and has already killed her son and grandson. The first thing she does is get dolled up and then positions herself where they can see each other. Some people suggest that she was trying to call upon her god to help her seduce Jehu while others say she wanted to make sure she was always seen as a queen. The second option makes less sense because she was already around servants that day because they reported to her. She wasn't dressing for a ball or to meet with royalty from other nations. She was preparing for the next man in charge.

Narcissists are known for their sexual perversions. They tend to be extremely sexual and promiscuous, especially to get favors. They are undercover prostitutes. Some of their tactics include openly talking about theirs and others' sexual conquests in front of anyone, especially children. They usually have an extensive pornography collection and will leave toys, pictures, and movies in places where they can be found or least expected, such as on the living room shelf with family movies. They have no problem watching X-rated movies with their children and grandchildren. Narcissists have been known to be exhibitionists and walk around their children of the opposite sex with breasts and genitals exposed and will use excuses to have them come to the parent while naked. They love talking about body parts, how they look, their children's sex organs, their children's sex lives, and will offer instructions on how "it should be done." Some narcissists are also child molesters and rapists because they feel they're above the law and entitled to do whatever they want with their children and their children's bodies.

Narcissists love to take pictures of themselves and think everyone believes they are the most beautiful and sexiest things to walk the earth. They are always ready for a camera and want to stand out as the best looking one in the picture or, at least, the focal point. Pictures are numerous and are usually meant to show body parts. The ones meant to be seductive are usually obvious, like pushing breasts into a camera or posing with legs spread apart for no reason other than to show they're sexually available.

Threats/Intimidation tactics

"[31]And as Jehu entered in at the gate, she said, Had Zimri peace, who slew his master?" – 2 Kings 9:31

Zimri was a captain in the army of King Elah of Israel. The Lord had told the prophet Jehu that Baasha's line would be removed from the throne and wiped out; however, Zimri was never instructed by God to kill anyone (1 Kings 16:1-20). Zimri killed Baasha's family and took over as king – for seven days. Omri, Ahab's father and Jezebel's father-in-law, was voted king. Omri went after Zimri, and Zimri committed suicide by fire.

Jezebel is well informed about Israel's history, especially since Zimri was the king prior to her husband's family dynasty being established. Zimri committed suicide to avoid being killed by Omri, which means he did not live to enjoy taking the throne from the king. It seems that Jezebel is saying that Jehu will certainly die if he kills her. Although the Lord had given prophecies against Baasha and against Ahab that the thrones would be taken and men killed, Jezebel is still fighting against the inevitable. She is trying to intimidate him to get him to stop in the middle of what he's doing. Jehu has already killed two kings, and Jezebel knows he's coming for her when she yells to him. She's trying to save her own life. Getting prettied up didn't slow him down, so she used another tactic to make him fearful and save herself.

Narcissists are masters at intimidation tactics and will often send threats. They will use it on people who are smaller or in less powerful positions than themselves, such as against their children, as well as against people who are more powerful. Jehu was technically king because he had been anointed by God. Narcissists will use a bad example to try to make you change the course on which God set you, especially when it means the narcissist would be dethroned.

No contact

Notice that there is no record that Elijah ever talked directly to Jezebel. For all we know, the two were never even in the same space together. The only conversation with Jezebel involving Elijah is when Ahab reports to her about Baal losing on Mt. Carmel. For the remainder of Elijah's ministry and until Elisha is instructed to send someone to anoint Jehu to kill Jezebel, everyone stays away from Jezebel except those serving her.

Narcissists are walking explosives. Unless and until confrontation becomes necessary, it is best to stay away. Narcissists drag people down into their pit of evil. As shown in Revelation 2, those who choose to play with or follow her example and ways will be destroyed as well for their choices.

Do not engage Jezebel

"[32]And he lifted up his face to the window, and said, Who is on my side? who? And there looked out to him two or three eunuchs." – 2 Kings 9:32

Jezebel asks him about Zimri to scare Jehu and make him change his mind about his assignment. Instead of arguing with her, he doesn't even acknowledge that she spoke. He called out to the people near her to ask who was on his side. Two or three eunuchs look out of the window to let him know they were with him.

There's a bit of irony here with the eunuchs. They were in service to the queen/queen mother, but men were often castrated if they were around the queen so that they could not make sexual advances. At the same time, they usually had little or no sexual desires. None of her charms or sexual advances would work on them. Whatever she thought might work on Jehu didn't faze them.

Narcissists are notorious for arguing, yelling, accusing, talking in circles, bringing up irrelevant topics, and trying to distract you from your goal. It is a waste of time to play on their level because you are playing in Satan's court. They want the argument and the fight. They want to deter you from anything that isn't beneficial to and focused on themselves. They want you to become weary and broken down trying to explain something to them or defend yourself. The argument is meant to put you off balance and make you react. It is a lost cause to argue or engage them and try to have a rational conversation with them. The one interaction we see with someone trying to give an explanation results in Jezebel vowing revenge and hurling death threats.

Jezebel must be evicted

We do not know exactly how long Jezebel was around, but she had to be in the picture at least three decades based on the 14 years combined total of her sons' reigns plus their getting into power at least in their late teens, if not at older ages. After she got Ahab to do what she wanted, she began to extend her reach into the Southern Kingdom through marrying off her daughter (or pimping her, depending on how you read it), and she reigned through her sons.

"[33]And he said, Throw her down. So they threw her down:" – 2 Kings 9:33a

"[20]Notwithstanding I have a few things against thee, *because thou sufferest that woman Jezebel*," – Revelation 2:20a – They were permitting or allowing her to continue teaching in the church and leading the people of Christ into grave sins.

Jezebel feeds on money, power, and control, and she will *not* walk away. She must be forcibly removed from her position. In this case, she was hurled out of a window.

Narcissists either must face a legal consequence because of their damage, or we have to minimize or eliminate interaction with them. This is one of the reasons so many people benefit from going "no contact" with the narcissist, enablers, and anyone on the strings of the narcissist puppet master. The victims save themselves stress and simultaneously reduce the power narcissists have in their lives. They are taking control of their individual kingdoms (families) and preventing narcissists from contaminating all the people under their reach.

Jezebel refuses to repent

"[21]And I gave her space to repent of her fornication; and she repented not." – Revelation 2:21

Jesus said this of spiritual Jezebel or the person with a Jezebel spirit. When we look at Original Jezebel, we see that she never acknowledges her wrongdoings. She has been operating behind the scenes and pulling strings for at least 30 years, yet she *never* repents or even accepts accountability for her sins. As she faced imminent death, she held onto her sins and took them with her into hell.

Narcissists do not apologize. They mean what they do and mean what they say. Every stunt is calculated. They don't care who they hurt.

They don't care about who dies in the process of them achieving their objectives. *This is one place in which the narcissist is truthful because she means every destructive thing she has ever done to you.* Therefore, she will not repent.

The closest to an apology that you will get is projection – when she accuses you of things she has done or is doing. The next runner up is, "I'm sorry that you think I did something wrong" or a similar phrase that means it's your fault that you're upset because the narcissist clearly believes she has never done anything wrong. She never shows remorse. She never attempts to hear you out and empathize to understand how her actions harmed you. She will blow it off and turn the tables on you for ever stating that her actions bothered you, because you cannot put her in any negative light – ever.

Remember, Jezebel lived to see or hear about:

1. Miracles – no rain or dew for years, the Lord won the showdown at Mt. Carmel, fire from Heaven killed two sets of fifty army men, the Lord providing water when armies went out to battle, wild animals, Naaman cured of leprosy
2. Prophecies fulfilled – If she knew about Elijah's prophecies, she could see that the five men in her immediate family died according to the Word of God.

None of these things moved her.

The Lord showed His mercy to His enemies throughout this family's rule. We saw that God showed mercy to a Zidonian woman who believed Him, which tells us that Jezebel's background didn't matter. Even people from Zidon who had been raised in idol worship would be accepted if they believed on Him. The Lord granted the Shunammite woman a child and healed the army commander of Israel's enemy from an incurable disease, which shows us that God extends grace and mercy to non-Jews. He also didn't allow the Syrian army to be killed or even leave hungry when they were led into Samaria after being temporarily blinded when they came after Elisha. This shows us the Lord still shows compassion to enemies and gives people time to correct their ways.

Jezebel had at least 30 years to repent and give up her ways to acknowledge the Lord. She refused even when she was about to have her Divine sentence carried out.

Narcissists have opportunities to do right. The only way they will change is by giving up their ways for the Lord. It is possible (ex. King Nebuchadnezzar), but since narcissists are their own gods, they often will not humble themselves. The proud will not come to God, and God resists the proud since they usually behave as if they do not need Him. If miracles, recent history, and multiple prophecies do not move Jezebel, your attempt to persuade her through eloquent speech and convincing points will never mean anything to her. Only the Lord can change the narcissist, but the narcissist must be willing to humble herself and repent.

<u>Jezebel is unwanted</u>

Jehu didn't have to storm the king's home or use a sales pitch to talk people into following him. When his companions heard that he was anointed king and would then need to kill the present king, they joyfully embraced him as king and set out immediately to secure it. The eunuchs only needed one invitation to throw the queen to her death. The Bible tells us her blood got on the walls and the horses. Jehu drove his chariot over her body and then went to eat. A skull, hands, and feet remained of her, and not a single person seemed upset.

The narcissist is an evil person who makes life miserable for those she's near. Even the person with the smallest position/status jumps at the opportunity to be rid of her for good. Sadly, some have been severely abused by the narcissist and have developed an intense hatred for the narcissist in their lives. Due to the constant turmoil being caused, victims may dream of days when the narcissist dies. I have heard many people say they don't even want to attend the abuser's funeral. The level of trauma inflicted on victims is so severe that many feel they can't fully be at peace until their tormentors finally die. This is not because they want to see the narcissist killed. Rather, the extent of the damage is so far-reaching and continues because she refuses to stop meddling, so victims feel their suffering will not cease until the narcissist is no longer able to do or say anything to add to the problems caused while alive.

Jehu Utterly Destroys the House of Ahab and Baal Worship

2 Kings 10

Summary

Jehu sent letters to the elders, rulers, and those who brought up and watched the 70 sons of Ahab and told them to find the best of his sons and prepare to fight for the kingdom. The elders decided that they should side with Jehu since he'd just killed two kings. Jehu told them to prove their loyalty by killing the former king's sons. After a time, Jehu reminded the people of Elijah's prophecy regarding the house of Ahab. Jehu killed the remaining allies, relatives, and priests of Ahab as well as the 42 male relatives of Ahaziah (deceased king of Judah) who entered the capital of Israel, Samaria.

Jehu and a man he encountered, Jehonadab, told everyone that Jehu wanted to proclaim a big worship ceremony for Baal and that anyone who follows Baal should attend. Once they packed the temple, they worshiped while Jehu gave instructions to the guards he placed around it. They killed all the Baal priests and worshipers, broke the images, and destroyed the temple to eliminate that religion from Israel. Jehu was told that God would see that Jehu's descendants would reign until the fourth generation for his zeal in obedience; however, Jehu didn't completely follow the Lord and would slip into idolatry later.

What we see here:

Golden children/Ahab had more than 2 sons
Irony of the ceremonies

Golden Children/Ahab's 70 Sons:

While sons and brethren can include people studying or in a close group as well as relatives, as it does when speaking of Ahaziah (remember Jehoram of Judah's wives and sons except Ahaziah were taken and killed), it doesn't fit here given the fact that we had so

90

much detail about two of his sons. It is also likely that Jezebel was just one of his wives and that her actions were so heinous that the Bible had to include her deeds along with those of her husband and sons because of the international destruction caused. We do not see anything that specifies that Ahaziah and Jehoram were the two eldest sons. We know they walked in the ways of Ahab and Jezebel. Given Jezebel's tight grip on Ahab and her lust to kill for power, it appears that she made sure that her children, or her preferred children, would be seated on the throne over the other 70.

This small glimpse into the family may be viewed as selecting the "golden child." This is the child who receives better treatment than his siblings but still part of the narcissist's plan. The favorite child is chosen to help the parent stay on a pedestal, used as an enabler, and sometimes become narcissists themselves. In Jezebel's case, she needed one of her biological children on the throne after her husband died so that she could continue ruling from behind the curtain.

Proclaim a solemn ceremony

Even though Jezebel had just been killed, I find justice in the route Jehu took to do the same thing Jezebel did. He proclaimed a special religious ceremony to be held for Baal, a god he didn't worship just as she didn't worship the Lord. He arranged for special robes to be given and for everyone who worshiped to gather together so that they were made to feel special, as Naboth did, before they were killed. It is possible that some who participated in any of Jezebel's original worship and plots lived to have the tables turned on themselves in this ceremony. We won't know for sure during this lifetime, but it seems likely given that we're still talking about one generation and that God was paying back what people had dished out.

Terror: Athaliah's Rise and Fall

2 Kings 11

Parallel Passage 2 Chronicles 22:10 – 2 Chronicles 23:21

Summary

Recap: The activity in this chapter occurred just after chapter 9. Chapter 10 tells us what happened when Jehu took over in Israel. Chapter 11 tells us what happened in the Southern Kingdom of Judah. Remember that Athaliah married Jehoram. Jehoram murdered his brothers. His judgment from God included having his wives and children taken except for the youngest, Ahaziah – son of Athaliah. Ahaziah visited his injured uncle in Israel and was killed by Jehu when both kings (Jezebel's son and grandson) rode out to meet him.

Athaliah saw that her son, King Ahaziah, was dead, which meant that there was no king in Judah. One of his sons would be next in line to rule. She then proceeds to kill off the royal bloodline so that there is no heir to the throne. She then begins to reign as the only queen to sit on the throne in Jewish history. She reigned because no one knew the only grandchild to escape the slaughter had been hidden. Jehosheba is Ahaziah's sister and aunt to her young nephew, Joash/Jehoash. She and her priest husband, Jehoiada, hide young Joash and his nurse in the temple of the Lord for several years.

Athaliah ruled for six years. When Joash was seven, Jehoiada gathered rulers and captains to make a covenant that they would be loyal to the Lord and David's bloodline so that they would protect the young heir. During a changing of the priests, they positioned themselves at the temple, blew trumpets, anointed him, sang praises to God, and proclaimed young Joash to be king. Athaliah went to see the commotion and cried out, "Treason! Treason!" before fleeing. She was allowed to leave the temple to avoid defiling it, and then she was executed. All who were loyal and protected her were killed. The images of Baal, his priest, and his temple were also destroyed.

Joash, at age seven, became the youngest king on the throne in Jewish history. The priest who reared him was his guide as he ruled. During that time, worship for the Lord returned.

What we see here:

Jezebels consider their children disposable
Jezebel's true goal is the throne
Jezebel is antichrist
Hypocrisy/Jezebel seeks false sympathy and support

Children are disposable

Repeat: Jezebels do not love anyone!

There is no record of Jezebel or Athaliah mourning for anyone – not even their children. What mother is not completely heartbroken when she learns her child has died? Both Jezebel and Athaliah watched their husbands die after the deaths were prophesied, and neither made any effort to contact the prophet to see if there was any way to prevent their children from suffering the same fate. Neither witch shed a tear upon learning that Jehu killed their sons. They simply began the next phase of their plans and stepped right into a position to rule. Their children were no more than objects required to accomplish their goals. While the names of Jehoram of Israel and the Ahaziahs suggested they exalted Jehovah, their actions said otherwise. They played the necessary roles to appear as if they cared about God's plan while living lifestyles in service to Baal. The women took on mother roles because they were continuing dynasties, but they clearly didn't like their children.

Athaliah is the Jezebel we see when she's given the opportunity to show what's really in her heart. She shows us what she really thinks about her children and grandchildren. She went on a cold-blooded murdering spree to *kill off her own grandchildren*! That is not the action of a person who "loves." In fact, it doesn't even seem that she realized she had missed a grandchild in her slaughter because there's no hunt for Joash after killing the others. Unlike the behavior of most grandmothers to visit with, hold, and try to see their grandchildren's "firsts," this grandmother didn't even seem to realize her grandchild existed. Jezebels hate their own offspring and would kill them if they saw a benefit from it.

Narcissists are known for being hateful and cruel to their children. For some reason, we believe they will change when they see their grandchildren. Clearly, they don't. Their grandchildren are still seen as extensions of themselves to be used as tools or indentured servants to do their bidding. Children and grandchildren are considered property. The narcissist will often admit that they believe they own their descendants and will act offended if told otherwise. They will demand to be put first in their children's lives, expect to be given money and property when demanded, expect preferential treatment on their children's birthdays, will take the spotlight from their children, expect lifetime loyalty, and demand access to every aspect of their lives. They punish grown children as if they're under age 10 for "backtalk," standing up for themselves, making decisions without the narcissist's input, or not caving in to their every whim. Children of narcissists tend to seriously consider suicide multiple times, and their parents may only try to persuade them to stick around because the child is still needed for tasks such as paying the mortgage on their house.

<u>Jezebel wants to rule over everyone</u>

Original Jezebel ruled through her husband and sons. Two-fold child of hell Jezebel, Athaliah, went straight for the crown as soon as she saw the opportunity. Her son-king was just killed according to Elijah's prophecy. How does the mother react? She decides it would be best if she went around and killed her grandchildren, too. Her purpose in doing this was not to beat Jehu to the punch of killing Ahaziah's descendants because that was never the plan. Israel wasn't the legitimate kingdom to eventually give way to the Christ. The reason she killed off the royal house was to prevent anyone from challenging her right to reign. By eliminating heirs to the throne, she eliminates the middlemen and doesn't have to convince the king to do things her way. She just gives the direct order as the queen.

Absolute rule and unrivaled authority are the ultimate goals of Jezebel because it means others are forced to submit to their control.

It comes with numerous flatterers, a captive audience, and the ability to destroy at will.

Narcissists seek this on multiple levels through their lives because precious few will ever have the opportunity to wield this kind of national power. They will use whatever sneaky tactics they can to knock others out of the way to achieve their goals – even if it means crushing their own children and grandchildren in the process.

Jezebel is antichrist

She is against God. *Athaliah is **not** an atheist*! None of these people were atheists. Athaliah behaved as if she was a god. She was against the Lord God. She played along, too, like her mother did. Original Jezebel knew the Law of Moses and the history of the people as well as she knew her Baal worship and practices. Athaliah had the ability to do more damage in the Southern Kingdom of Judah because she married into the royal dynasty of King David. Everyone knew the prophecy from Genesis of the Promised Redeemer. Jacob/Israel had prophesied about Christ coming through the kingly line of Judah. The Lord had promised David that his lineage would continue and that Christ would come through his genealogy.

Why is that important? What does that have to do with Athaliah?

It means: *Not only was Athaliah's killing spree meant to eliminate anyone who could rival her for the throne, **it meant that she intended to prevent the coming of Jesus Christ – the Messiah!***

Let's recap:

1. Jehoshaphat, descendant of David and a Godly king, allowed Jehoram to co-reign with him because he would rule next.
2. Jehoram married Athaliah and began following Baal.
3. Jehoram killed his brothers, so he was the only son left of Jehoshaphat.
4. Jehoram's sin led to his wives and sons being taken and killed. The sole surviving child was Ahaziah, which means Ahaziah is considered Jehoram's only son and Jehoshaphat's only grandson.

5. Ahaziah is killed. When kings die, the rule of the kingdom usually goes to a son (the reason Ahab's second son took over in Israel when the first died – the first had no sons).
6. Jehoshaphat's great-grandson should have been next in line. However, Athaliah decided to destroy the entire line and end the dynasty with herself.

(This is also an issue with narcissists changing their wills to make sure their children inherit nothing as a last means of control.)

Athaliah didn't care about her lineage and legacy. She didn't kill off the royal family to prevent someone from killing them first; otherwise, she would have committed suicide to die with everyone else. Athaliah wanted to cut off the hope of the people of God. Had she been successful, she would have made God look like a liar, turned hearts from the Lord, and ultimately, removed all hope of salvation from everyone who ever lived. She was satanic to the core.

However, God preserved a remnant.

Joash was saved by his aunt and hidden in the last place Athaliah would think to look – the temple of the Lord. He was the grandson of Athaliah, sole surviving great-grandson of Jehoshaphat, and the descendant of David who would continue the bloodline of the dynasty that would be counted in the ancestral lineage of Christ.

Again, the narcissist wants to destroy anyone who is righteous and a follower of the Lord.

"Treason! Treason!" – Poor Me

Hypocritical, isn't it?

Here is a woman who murdered her grandchildren for the sole purpose of taking over the throne and denying rightful heirs opportunity to rule. And now she has the nerve to yell and claim that the priests and guards are trying to overthrow proper and established authority and threaten her reign and life, even though she was never meant to occupy the position. It seems to be an irrational argument, but it's actually a cunning last-ditch effort to keep her status by confusing the people present. By yelling and tearing her clothes, she gives the impression that there was a subversive plot to overthrow the crown to put an illegitimate person in place. Royalty ripped their clothes to show mourning and great sorrow when some grave sin had been committed. The action would likely cause people to question the priests because Athaliah has portrayed herself as the victim instead of the perpetrator of all the problems. It can even be seen as disorienting the listeners. She came across as if others were unfairly targeting her. The focal switch was so swift and subtle that, unless you were privy to the information in the story as we are, because we can read it, you might not notice the people attending were forced to shift thoughts from the anointing of a king to the idea that there was a secret coup to overthrow the queen. This actually puts the innocent people doing the right thing in the position of defending themselves and their actions.

Again, we see Jezebel fails to own her wrongs. She actually blames and endangers the lives of others to protect her lies/sins.

Have you ever been involved in a conversation or confrontation with the narcissist about something, and they switch subjects when you have a strong, valid point? This switch is meant to throw you and other listeners off balance to make you believe what they say or is meant to make you back down. You could be reminding them that they agreed and signed to pay a debt, and they will ask you why you didn't pay for your portion of a meal they purchased two weeks ago. Narcissists will challenge you for challenging them or putting them on the spot in front of other people. If there is an audience, and the narcissist stands to lose face in front of them, the narcissist will get loud, put on a display or become highly dramatic/histrionic, and find a way to deflect negative attention from them back to you as if you are the guilty party.

This is also when you will see "crocodile (empty) tears" from the narcissist. For instance, your narcissist may have cursed you out, told you to let her be by herself to heal, and stopped taking her medicine because she's going to "treat" herself. When you and other visitors show up, she starts crying about how no one cares about her, starts accusing you of trying to poison her by passing her the wrong meds, and blames you for leaving her to die. The narcissist uses any opportunity to pass blame to someone else to avoid bearing responsibility and accountability.

Conclusion: Take Your Life Back

This study has been the most physically exhausting study I have ever attempted. It's not that it was overly complicated. It was emotionally tiring as I recognized how these tactics had been used and played out against me. I find that when we try to explain the things we've experienced and then explain why we were still involved with people, it's hard to get listeners to grasp the invisible chain we feel we have on us. Hopefully, others who are unaware of this type of stealth abuse will read and learn how narcissists operate while offering a more sympathetic ear.

There are a few things that I remind myself:

1. Even though your abuse may have been done in secret, there is One Who is aware of everything that has happened. Your narcissist will not be able to fast talk her way out of answering to God.
2. We cannot truly begin to heal until we know the root cause of our conditions and/or why we have the challenges we do. Putting a bandage on a gaping sore does you no good in the long term. You have to find the origin of the infection, clean it out, and treat it accordingly. We must do the same to address emotional issues such as why we excuse the behavior of the person routinely and purposely hurting us when we wouldn't make that excuse for a person beating someone with a baseball bat.
3. The sadness I occasionally feel isn't about missing the person but mourning the relationship and memories that never happened.

For most of us who care deeply, it is hard to walk away from the narcissist or the enabler tied to the narcissist because we're hoping that if we hold on just a little bit longer, they will see the light. You cannot "love" the narcissist into hurting you less. I know this seems odd to many Believers because we want to believe "love conquers all." We can love people, including enemies, and not put ourselves in the position of being doormats. Jezebels are antichrists at heart, so trying to win them with "love" won't work. The reason it doesn't work is that they are completely sold out to another god. They can only respond with evil or mimic goodness with an evil ulterior motive.

Narcissists cannot be "treated" by therapy or medication. This individualized attention only offers them an audience whereby they can project the version of themselves that will garner sympathy and put them in the best light. This person is not suffering from a brain injury, a chemical imbalance, or the inability to distinguish between good and bad choices. This is not a disorder where the person is seeing demons and is terrified because she does not want them there. This is the person who has committed herself to delete, destroy, or dispose of anyone who does not give her what she wants. She is not "incapable" of doing right or sympathizing. She chooses not to do so. She does not care about what happens to others because she has allowed her conscience to become "seared." She is practically a walking demon. Still, she has no excuse.

Without a heart change like that of King Nebuchadnezzar of Babylon when he acknowledged the Lord and humbled himself, these folks will not change. That means that unless they ask for God to change them, none of our actions are going to move them. Remember, Jezebel saw miracles with her own eyes, watched the prophet's words play out multiple times in her life, and refused to repent even when she faced imminent death. She was given space to repent but would not. As a Christian, the most loving thing we can do is give them the truth and then let them make their own choices. If they don't want God to change them and release them from their hatred, they certainly don't want to receive anything from anyone else.

So, what should we do?

I think the first thing we should do is recognize that we were targeted and attacked. We should honestly consider our part in any interaction, but it doesn't erase years of abuse. We need to stop taking the blame for other people's choice to behave with evil intent. If we need to repent for anything we have done, then we do so and ask God to work in us so that we can heal.

We should not entertain the narcissist. In both Old and New Testaments, the Lord never instructed His people to argue, have deep conversations, or try to persuade Jezebel to do or stop doing anything. She is completely aware of what she is doing and is causing harm to people as long as we allow her a place to operate in our lives. In some cases, we can simply go "no contact" and cut all interaction with her the same way we saw Elijah never spoke to her. That means we can simply stop calling, texting, hanging out with them, etc. In other cases, it is necessary to remove them from their positions, even if it means the position in our homes. That may mean putting a relative out or removing a Jezebel from a position in the church. The reason is that people who are not aware of her dangers will follow her. Allowing her to lead and give them guidance will cause them to partake in her judgment and destruction. Jezebel, her husband, sons, daughter, son-in-law, grandson, and dozens of other relatives were all brought to a shameful end, written in history as one of the most wicked families of Israel, died under the judgment of God, sparked people to rejoice at their deaths, and are now in hell.

"[20]Notwithstanding I have a few things against thee, because thou sufferest that woman Jezebel, which calleth herself a prophetess, to teach and to seduce my servants to commit fornication, and to eat things sacrificed unto idols. [21]And I gave her space to repent of her fornication; and she repented not. [22]Behold, I will cast her into a bed, and them that commit adultery with her into great tribulation, except they repent of their deeds. [23]And I will kill her children with death; and all the churches shall know that I am he which searcheth the reins and hearts: and I will give unto every one of you according to your works." – Revelation 2:20-23

For those under our care, such as our children, we have a responsibility to protect them and not allow narcissists to lure them into their traps and teach them wrongly. In the natural, it can cause much pain, heartache, broken families, sickness, and death. In the spiritual, allowing impressionable listeners to sit under Jezebel's teachings will lead them to the same fate as Baal worship because it still leads away from the true God. It has a more permanent and eternal consequence. It really is a spiritual battle, and it's one that Jezebel always loses. We do not need to get dragged down with her.

Thankfully, we are becoming more aware to recognize the actions of Jezebel and to offer support for her victims. Some ways people have begun the process of healing is by doing as much research as they can on the topic, listening to testimonies of others, attended counseling from therapists who are familiar with the personality disorder, etc. You may choose some or all of these options. The biggest thing is to recognize what you have experienced, acknowledge it, and choose to recover. Do not allow people who never cared about you to convince you that you "will never" do what you were meant to do.

You have value.

You are important.

Your feelings are valid.

Your abuse shouldn't be swept under the rug and ignored.

You don't have to subject yourself to more suffering.

You are not alone in this. There is a growing community of survivors dedicated to helping you recover and regain your voice that was silenced by predators. Decide today that yesterday was your last day in bondage to your Jezebel. Set your goal, and begin your plans to protect yourself and your loved ones. If necessary, contact a local abuse center to help you develop a plan to safely exit your situation.

For both survivors and those in the position to stop or prevent abuse, I have one message:

"Do not tolerate Jezebel!"

About the Author

Miko Marsh is a mother, author, caregiver, instructor, and motivator. She earned a Bachelor of Science degree in Psychology from Old Dominion University and a college certification in Early Childhood Care Education from Chattahoochee Technical College. She has worked directly with individuals in behavioral facilities and owned her own daycare.

Miko has authored several books related to caregiving, an educational workbook for introduction to childcare training, and a book on personal transformation. Her many articles, blogs, blurbs, and notes can be found online at different ministries, organizations, and businesses for which she was a contributor or ghostwriter. Miko's interest areas include Bible-based topics, caregiving, personal growth, and interpersonal communications. However, she has been known to write things to amuse herself because she also loves to laugh.

In addition to homeschooling her children, she has given instruction in piano, reading music, mathematics, and other areas in which she could assistant. She enjoys supporting others, helping them to find areas in which they can shine, and seeing people of all ages and abilities reach their individual goals.

Other books by this author

I truly appreciate you reading my book! If you enjoyed it, please take a moment to leave a review. You can also find me on other platforms.

Subscribe to Youtube: Miko Moments channel

Website: http://www.mikomoments.com

Please visit your favorite ebook retailer to discover other books by Miko Marsh:

Stop Surviving and Live! How I Changed My Poverty Mindset to Control My Future

Daycare Days for Providers: What You Should Know before Opening Your Home

Daycare Days for Parents: Answers & Tips from a Provider

Introduction to Childcare: An Overview for the Aspiring Professional Caregiver (coming soon)

Made in the USA
Middletown, DE
27 March 2018